Gregory J. Cra

Negotiating Buck Naked: Doukhobors, Public Policy, and Conflict Resolution

UBCPress · Vancouver · Toronto

15 14 13 12 11 10 09 08 07 06   5 4 3 2 1

Printed in Canada on acid-free paper

Library and Archives Canada Cataloguing in Publication

Cran, Gregory
   Negotiating buck naked : Doukhobors, public policy, and conflict resolution /
Gregory J. Cran.

Includes bibliographical references and index.
ISBN-13: 978-0-7748-1258-0 (bound); 978-0-7748-1259-7 (pbk.)
ISBN-10: 0-7748-1258-3 (bound); 0-7748-1259-1 (pbk.)

   1. Sons of Freedom Doukhobors – British Columbia. 2. Dukhobors –
Government policy – British Columbia. 3. Dukhobors – Civil rights – British
Columbia. 4. Conflict management – British Columbia – Case studies.
5. Dukhobors – Canada – History. 6. Dukhobors – Canada – Government
relations. I. Title.

FC3850.D76C72 2006   305.6'899   C2006-900067-0

Canadä

UBC Press gratefully acknowledges the financial support for our publishing
program of the Government of Canada through the Book Publishing Industry
Development Program (BPIDP), and of the Canada Council for the Arts, and
the British Columbia Arts Council.

This book has been published with the help of a grant from the Canadian
Federation for the Humanities and Social Sciences, through the Aid to Scholarly
Publications Programme, using funds provided by the Social Sciences and
Humanities Research Council of Canada.

UBC Press
The University of British Columbia
2029 West Mall
Vancouver, BC V6T 1Z2
604-822-5959 / Fax: 604-822-6083
www.ubcpress.ca

Contents

Acknowledgments

This is a project that started twenty-five years ago when I first began working with the Doukhobor communities in the West Kootenay and Boundary regions, which are located in the south-central part of British Columbia. The genesis of my encounter with the Doukhobor people goes back even further, to when I was twelve years old and living in the town of Hope, British Columbia. This is where I first encountered the Sons of Freedom Doukhobors who had arrived at our school after having trekked some 485 kilometres. This was where I met Alex Zaitsoff (now deceased), who shared a locker with me up until the day, about three months later, when he, his family, and the rest of their community left to continue their trek.

Over these past many years there are some whom I wish to thank for having challenged and inspired my thinking. These include Hugh Herbison and Tom McGauley, who introduced me to Kootenay life and Doukhobor lore thirty-four years ago; Dr. Joseph Schaeffer, whose work in community and communication is truly insightful and cutting edge; and Dr. Marie Hoskins, who helped me realize that the postmodern view of the world isn't as scary as some make it out to be.

My special note of thanks goes to Fred Makortoff, Jim Popoff, Steve Lapshinoff, and many others in the Doukhobor community for opening their world to me by sharing their stories and their perceptions. I also thank Jack McIntosh, Derryl White, Dr. Mel Stangeland, Dr. Mark Mealing, and Ron Cameron, who served as members of the Kootenay Committee on Intergroup Relations for eight years, and the late Robin Bourne, who kept us all in line.

Finally, I wish to thank Jean Wilson and Darcy Cullen at UBC Press; my two sons – Rob and Joel – who kept me going with their humour, their discoveries, and their patience when I needed space or time to be alone; my wife Katherine, whose endless support helped me realize that tall mountains are climbable once you have them in your sights; and the angel that sat on my shoulder and kept reminding me that I needed to finish what I was doing before moving on. It is memories such as these that shape who we are in the stories we become.

Organizations and Acronyms

Agassiz Mountain Prison   Opened in July 1962 to house approximately seventy Sons of Freedom sentenced for bombing and arson.

CCBRD   Christian Community and Brotherhood of Reformed Doukhobors. These were former Sons of Freedom who, starting in the 1950s, chose to follow Stephan Sorokin.

CCUB Ltd.   Christian Community of Universal Brotherhood Limited. This organization was incorporated in 1917 and continued to operate until 1938, when it went into receivership.

Consultative Committee on Doukhobor Affairs   The committee was chaired by Dr. Geoff Andrew of the University of British Columbia. It consisted of representatives from the Doukhobor communities, both the federal and the provincial governments, and the Royal Canadian Mounted Police.

Doukhobor Research Committee   This committee was formed in 1950 after the collapse of the Sullivan Commission in 1948. It was chaired by Dr. Harry Hawthorn of the University of British Columbia.

EKCIR   Expanded Kootenay Committee on Intergroup Relations. This committee was launched in October 1982.

KCIR   Kootenay Committee on Intergroup Relations. This committee was established in November 1979.

Piers Island   Commissioned as a federal penitentiary from 1932 to 1935 in order to house the 570 Sons of Freedom who were sentenced to three years for public nudity. Off the southern tip of Vancouver Island.

Society Rodina   Formerly the Committee for Cultural Relations with Russian Descendants Abroad.

USCC   Union of Spiritual Communities of Christ. This organization was made up of Orthodox Doukhobors and was registered as a society in 1957.

Negotiating Buck Naked

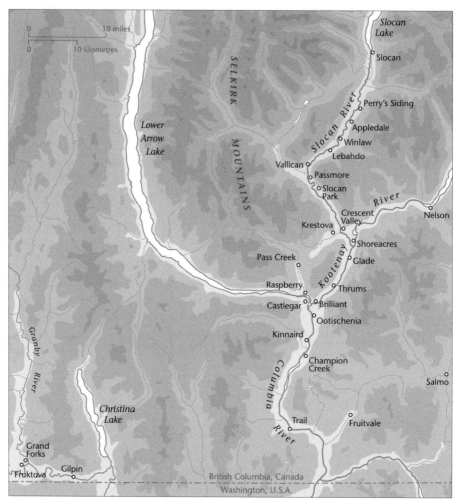

British Columbia Doukhobor settlements, Boundary and West Kootenay districts, 1908 to present. *Map by Eric Leinberger, adapted from map by J. Kalmakoff*

1
Introduction

While I pondered what he said, he leaned toward me as if to
speak in confidence. "Let me give you one piece of advice ...
you can't apply rational thinking to an irrational situation."[1]

In 1899 a group of Russian peasants referred to as the Doukhobors im-
migrated to Canada after having suffered centuries of persecution in
Russia. Soon after their arrival conflict emerged between these new immigrants and the state over such issues as land ownership, the registration of births and deaths, and school attendance. As positions hardened,
a splinter group known as the Sons of Freedom emerged, and it used
public nudity, arson, and bombings as a means of both protest and
retaliation. These practices continued for the better part of a century.

Throughout the time the Doukhobors spent in Canada, numerous
unsuccessful attempts were made to address the conflict between them
and the state. These ranged from increased sanctions and long prison
terms to the apprehension of Sons of Freedom children and their six-
year confinement in a residential school setting. Over this long, tortu-
ous history, three commissions of inquiry were held (in 1912, 1947,
and 1956); a group of scholars studied the situation (1949); and, with
400 Sons of Freedom jailed, the University of British Columbia (UBC)
brought the Orthodox Doukhobor (also known as Community Doukhobor) leadership and Sons of Freedom together with the provincial
government in search of a solution (1950). All of this was to no avail.
Then, in 1979, a different type of intervention was tried (see below)
and, six years later, resulted in an accord. The question is, why did this
intervention work when others failed? What were the factors that led to
change?

This is a story that examines the events that, in 1979, brought together a skilled group of dedicated local non-Doukhobor people – the Kootenay Committee on Intergroup Relations (KCIR) – with the Doukhobor factions and a group of government officials and police. This group heard witnesses describe how bombing and arson came to be used as a means of protest and retaliation and how, over a period of sixty years, this was sometimes encouraged and sometimes discouraged by the Doukhobor leadership.

In examining the factors that led to change, my analysis draws upon interviews with key spokespersons for the Doukhobors, who played strategic roles in helping their groups bring an end to bombing and arson. The interviews explore these people's pasts and the stories they told about other groups and the government. They also explore how meaning was constructed and how the epiphanies that were experienced during the KCIR sessions reshaped people's perceptions and views of each other. The lessons resulting from this study challenge conventional conflict theory and conflict intervention practices.

My role dates back to 1978, when I was asked by the Ministry of the Attorney General of British Columbia to design an intervention process that, so I reasoned at the time, would focus attention away from provincial government. I was in my late twenties and I had to face an elderly group of extremely determined, very religious people who, at least with regard to the Sons of Freedom, had spent a good part of their lives in prison for standing up for what they believed. Notwithstanding our age difference and my role with the provincial government (which they viewed as the "devil"), we reached an accord. For the next twenty years I watched from a distance to see whether this agreement would hold, periodically wondering why the process had enabled the occurrence of such a dramatic change. Finally, I found my excuse to return to the region, this time as a doctoral student, eager to look for answers.

Outline of the Book

My purpose in telling this story is twofold: first, to fill a gap in the history of the Doukhobors regarding how, after many years of turmoil, competing narratives were eventually negotiated into a new story structure that laid the foundation for bringing an end to violence; second, to inform those interested in conflict intervention and peace building – whether they are government policy makers, police officers, conflict practitioners, or members of the general public – about the lessons that were learned in addressing a particularly complex ethno-political conflict. In short, I examine prevailing assumptions about conflict and conflict resolution models and look at how these unravel when confronted by a non-linear ethno-political conflict situation.

In Chapter 1, I provide a brief history of the Doukhobors and the conflicts that emerged when they came to Canada. I describe the various failed attempts on the part of the government and the community to address the ongoing tension between state policies and religious beliefs.

In Chapter 2, I explore what has been written about the Doukhobors and about conflict and culture. I do this in order to highlight not only where these theories diverge but also where their limitations come into play. In Chapter 3, I describe my role as a young provincial government representative who came face-to-face with a myriad of situations, ranging from hunger fasts and blockades to efforts to get all the groups in the same room together. In Chapter 4, I set out the conflicting narratives and events that unfolded in the period during which the KCIR was meeting.

In Chapter 5, I continue with the narrative exchange but note what happened when pressure was brought to bear on the Union of Communities of Christ, the Sons of Freedom, and the Fraternal Council of the Christian Community and Brotherhood of Reformed Doukhobors (also known as the "Reformed Sons of Freedom,") to make a choice between abandoning the process altogether and constructing a common narrative. I detail key parts of the exchange, the situations that emerged between sessions, and the dilemmas the groups faced in negotiating their storied pasts.

In Chapter 6, I return to the Kootenays after nearly twenty years to interview three people who played a significant role in helping the Orthodox Doukhobors and the Reformed Doukhobors reach an accord. I explore the meanings each group created about the other during their earlier years and then what happened when they participated in the KCIR sessions. In Chapter 7, those interviewed describe their experiences throughout the KCIR sessions and tell how these experiences helped them to reshape their views and perspectives.

Finally, in Chapter 8, I examine the transcripts and interviews to educe lessons that may be useful to conflict theorists and practitioners, public policy makers, and others addressing difficult and challenging conflict situations, such as that presented by the Doukhobors.

Historical Overview

The word "Doukhobor" is derived from the Russian term *Doukho-borets,* meaning "spirit wrestler" – a term applied in 1785 by Ambrosius, the

Archbishop of Ekaterinoslav, to a group of Russian peasants who left the Russian Orthodox Church. Although there are no written records to describe their origin, Tarasoff (1982) believes that the Doukhobors emanated from a schism that occurred as a result of changes in the liturgy introduced by the Patriarch Nikon in 1652. Those who left the church were known as the "Old Believers," and the Doukhobors were among them. However, it was not until the mid-1700s, when Sylvan Kolesnikoff, from the Ekaterinoslav province, denounced icon worship and opposed other church reforms that Doukhoborism took shape. It was at this time that many Doukhobors were exiled as the Tsarist government attempted to destroy the movement.

The Doukhobors became communally minded,[2] sharing all their possessions and working for the good of the community as a whole. By 1895 they were practising vegetarians and their pacifist tenets had led them to a complete break with the military. By burning all their firearms they dramatically demonstrated their refusal to kill. Their refusal to obey Russian conscription laws alienated them from the Tsarist government, which tried to destroy the sect through imprisonment, torture, and exile. By the end of the nineteenth century the Doukhobors sustained themselves with hopes and dreams of a "Promised Land," a place where they could live peacefully and practise their beliefs.

Peter Kropotkin, a Russian anarchist living in England, suggested that Canada would be a safe haven. Contacts were made with the Canadian government, which appeared sympathetic. A group headed by Aylmer Maude,[3] Prince Khilkov, and Doukhobor representatives Makhortoff and Ivin was delegated to find a suitable locality for resettlement.

The Doukhobor plight had become known in Britain through Leo Tolstoy, who garnered public support, particularly among the English Quakers, who empathized with the Doukhobors' situation. Enough funds were raised through the sale of Tolstoy's book, *Resurrection,* and other sources to enable the Doukhobors to immigrate to Canada in 1899. Initially 7,427 arrived, to be followed by an additional 417 between 1900 and 1920 (Hawthorn 1952, 8). The Canadian government granted the Doukhobors military exemption, just as it had done for the Mennonites.

The first contingent of Doukhobors to arrive settled on blocks of land in Saskatchewan (prior to 1905 the land upon which they settled was part of the Northwest Territories). Soon after their arrival, confusion arose when the federal government made it known that granting land title required individuals to sign a document and to swear an oath of allegiance to the Crown. Negotiations took place between the federal government and Doukhobor intermediaries, such as Aylmer Maude and James Mavor, which led to further confusion. The Doukhobors' communal lifestyle discouraged private ownership, thus most refused to sign for their land. This was the beginning of dissent within the ranks of the community.

In 1902 Peter Vasilievich Verigin,[4] known as Peter the Lordly, arrived in Canada anxious to cooperate with the government; he convinced all but a small number of families to sign for their land – a decision that caused discontent among those families who did not sign.[5] Although the majority believed their leader to be divinely inspired, many began to withdraw from the community to become "Independents." As well, a small group, made up in part of discontented families who called themselves *svobodniki* (Sons of Freedom), began to show their dissent by protesting in the nude. In 1903 this group of *svobodniki* marched in the nude to show their fellow Doukhobors and the authorities that they believed in *real* freedom; however, the authorities were not impressed and all the marchers were arrested and sentenced to three months in jail. After their release a number of the men set fire to a thrashing machine as a symbolic attack on materialism and science. They were promptly convicted of arson and sentenced to three years in jail (Tarasoff 1982).

Further land conflicts in Saskatchewan arose over the Doukhobors' rejection of "patenting," or buying, the land because this required them to swear an oath of allegiance. This resulted in their being divested of much of the land upon which they had settled. This led Peter Verigin to purchase land privately in south-central British Columbia. This private purchase allowed him to hold land on behalf of his members and to do so without having to swear an oath of allegiance or to comply with the rigorous terms set out in the Homestead Act.

Starting in 1908 many Saskatchewan Doukhobors made their move to British Columbia. Soon after they arrived, new conflicts emerged, this time with the BC government, when families refused to register births and deaths with the Department of Vital Statistics and also refused to send their children to school. Parents who were fined refused to remit; as a counter measure the province passed the Community Regulation Act, 1914, which placed the onus of responsibility on every Doukhobor member to register births and deaths, to send each child to school, and to comply with the provisions of the Health Act. Those who violated the Community Regulation Act were to be fined, and if fines were not paid, then community assets could be seized (Tarasoff 1963).[6] To avert enforcement of this new legislation, Verigin made an agreement with the government whereby children would attend schools in their area (Tarasoff 1963). However, in 1920 amendments to the Public Schools Act created rural school districts, and this adversely affected the arrangements with the Doukhobors. If these new administrative arrangements were not adhered to, then not only could the community be forced to pay the full cost of the school and teachers' salaries but its assets could also be seized. By 1922 there were eleven schools established under this new arrangement, the government having built two and the others having been built by the Doukhobor community. The enrolment of Doukhobor children was 414, which represented approximately 82 percent of those children who would be considered school-age (Reid 1932). However, a steady drop in enrolment occurred as a result of this government-sponsored schools initiative. And in 1923 many schools were destroyed by fire.[7]

There were many other issues and events that led to unrest among the Doukhobors. In 1923 the Bolshevik government,[8] through its Technical Aid Society in New York, had persuaded a large group of Saskatchewan Doukhobors (approximately 2,000) to sell their property to two American companies whose principals would then assist them in their return to Russia, where they would help to implement a collective farming program. Lenin had long hoped for such a program, but so far it had not been successfully implemented. Sometime during this period Peter Verigin, upon hearing what was being planned, was able to divert attention away from this initiative to other migration plans. On 29 October 1924, between Castlegar and Grand Forks, a Canadian Pacific Railway passenger train was destroyed by an explosion that killed Verigin, along with eight other passengers, including a newly elected member of the provincial legislature.

There were many theories about what had caused the explosion, the three main ones being: (1) exploding pinch gas (the gas used in suspended pinch lamps for lighting the coaches), (2) unstable dynamite secretly brought aboard by a miner who was excavating in the area, and (3) a bomb planted by someone familiar with where the leader of the Doukhobors was sitting. The exploding pinch gas theory was ruled out due to the nature and extent of the damage, though some people still thought the railway company was concealing an accidental cause. The unstable dynamite theory was also ruled out given where the brunt of the damage occurred; that is, where Peter Verigin was sitting. The telling piece of evidence was a pocket watch found near the coach, with a copper connection soldered to one of the hands. Although this device had not been seen before, what became apparent later on was that similar technology was being used by the Sons of Freedom for detonating bombs. This is not to say that the Sons of Freedom were responsible for the train explosion but only that the bomb-making technology had been introduced by someone from outside the Doukhobor community.

The question that many would ask for generations to come is why would anyone want to assassinate Verigin? The Sons of Freedom believed the government had had him killed in order to end its troubles with the Doukhobors. Although there were many suspects, including an itinerant watchmaker who had arrived from the Soviet Union via Japan some months before, no one was ever convicted. This left the Sons of Freedom to suspect that Verigin's death was the result of a government conspiracy. This event marked the beginning of a long history of bombings, mainly directed at rail lines, bridges, and other rail and government facilities throughout the Kootenay and Boundary area.

In 1927 Peter Verigin's son, Peter Petrovich Verigin,[9] whom the Doukhobors referred to as *Chistiakov*, arrived from the Soviet Union to assume leadership of the Doukhobors. His leadership style and his untoward behaviour led many to wonder about him. Upon his arrival in Brilliant (a small town across the river from Castlegar) on 11 October 1927 he addressed those who had gathered to greet him. He referred to the Sons of Freedom as "the ringing bells" and praised them for not being "slaves of corruption." He described the Orthodox Doukhobors as being at a lesser spiritual level and criticized those who had left the Doukhobor community, calling them "Pharisees" and "materialists" who had been corrupted by the non-Doukhobor society. During his time in Canada (from 1927 to 1939)[10] the number of Sons of Freedom grew substantially, while the number of Orthodox Doukhobors decreased.[11] Also during his time here there was a significant decline in sawmill production and other revenue sources of the Christian Community of Universal Brotherhood Limited (CCUB Ltd.).[12] By 1938 sawmills fell into disuse as timber resources were exhausted and the last remaining productive mills in the Slocan Valley and Champion Creek were destroyed by fire.

In 1931 Peter Petrovich was convicted of perjury and sentenced to three years in prison in Prince Albert, Saskatchewan. Just prior to his conviction the federal government amended the offence provisions for public nudity under the Criminal Code, increasing the penalty from six months to three years in prison. Within the year over 600 Sons of Freedom were arrested in Nelson for nudity and were sentenced to three years in a makeshift penitentiary on Piers Island, located off the coast of Vancouver Island, across from Victoria. Their children, 365 in all, were placed in a variety of institutions and care facilities during their imprisonment.[13]

After Peter Petrovich completed only nine months of his sentence the federal government attempted to secretly deport him to the Soviet Union, presumably to rid itself of him. However, this attempt failed when a reporter for the *Saskatoon Star-Phoenix* newspaper got wind of Peter Petrovich's release and informed his lawyer, Peter Makaroff (who was also a Doukhobor but who was independent of the community). The federal government's deportation attempts came to a halt when the matter appeared before Justice Mellish, who ruled that Peter Petrovich was to be set free (Tarasoff 1982).

No sooner did Peter Petrovich get out of one scrape than he found himself in another. He sued his lawyer for overcharging him in the perjury case and condemned his other lawyer, Peter Makaroff, for over-charging him for his work during the perjury trial. In February 1934 Peter Petrovich was involved in a brawl in Nelson, then later that year he was involved in yet another brawl, this one in Winnipeg, where he was sentenced to two months in jail. After a number of years of self-abuse he was admitted to hospital for pains in his chest. Soon after entering hospital in Saskatoon, where he had infected ribs removed, he died of cancer on 11 February 1939 (Tarasoff 1982).

It was also in 1939 that the CCUB Ltd. went into receivership. Here the provincial government, in an effort to avert a mass eviction, purchased the debt owing to the mortgage holders, thus transferring the former CCUB Ltd. lands to the Crown. The newly acquired Crown lands were administered by the Provincial Land Settlement Board, which charged those continuing to live on the lands a nominal rental fee.

Following Peter Petrovich's death John J. Verigin, the grandson of Peter V. Verigin, assumed the mantle of leadership for the Orthodox Doukhobors, even though he was still in his late teens. This was to be an interim arrangement as the community waited for the arrival of Peter Verigin III, whom they referred to as *Yastrebov* (hawk), who was living somewhere in the Soviet Union. This was a particularly difficult time for young John J. as the community had just lost ownership of all of its lands, along with its main revenue source, and the social fabric that had held the community together for the past thirty years was quickly unravelling. This was the prelude to a period of rampant destruction, which began in 1940 when two community buildings were destroyed by fire.

During the 1940s efforts to enforce military service led to protests on the part of the Sons of Freedom. On 12 December 1943 a mass meeting was held between Doukhobors and representatives of the National Selective Service. By early next morning the jam factory, the general store, a packing shed, six boxcars, the gas station, and a garage in Brilliant had been destroyed by fire.[14] In January 1944 an unsuccessful attempt was made by twenty-two Doukhobors to burn John J. Verigin's residence in Brilliant, presumably because he was reported to be conferring with the National Selective Service in Vancouver.[15] Also during this period on four different occasions Peter V. Verigin's tomb was damaged by dynamite; eleven Doukhobor halls were destroyed by fire; and numerous Doukhobor villages, along with schools, Canadian Pacific Railway stations, homes, and other buildings, were set ablaze.[16]

In August 1947 there were a series of blazes throughout the Kootenay area, beginning with the burning of the home of John Lebedoff, who was a self-proclaimed leader of the Sons of Freedom. One hundred Sons of Freedom participated in its destruction. With the start of the Cold War, large numbers of people burned their own homes in protest over the possibility of a third world war. Tarasoff (1963) noted that many of these fires may have been "sacrificial fires," part of an initiation process associated with being inducted into the Sons of Freedom.

In addition to burning their own property, the Sons of Freedom burned two schools and eleven unoccupied houses in a former Japanese internment camp, and attempted to burn a community hall. In August of the same year, a number of Sons of Freedom made their way to Shoreacres, a Doukhobor and Sons of Freedom community located between Castlegar and Nelson on the north side of the Kootenay River, where they asked residents to remove all their furniture and belongings and join the cause. Again, numerous buildings and homes were destroyed by fire.

Similar actions were taken by those living in Gilpin, a small Sons of Freedom community located approximately thirteen kilometres east of Grand Forks on the Kettle River. The number of buildings destroyed by fire and explosives numbered in the several hundreds (Tarasoff 1963), and they included schools, several churches, many community homes, barns, factories, and public works. Throughout this period one person died in a fire in Krestova, and one man, who was guarding Peter V. Verigin's tomb, was shot in the hand, allegedly by Mike Bayoff, who later became a witness for the Crown and helped solve the many bombings that occurred throughout this period.

Numerous appeals were made to authorities to intervene, and in September 1947 Harry J. Sullivan, Judge of the County of New Westminster, was appointed commissioner of inquiry. At his first sitting in South Slocan on 14 October 1947 he said: "Canadian people are now determined to have a final show-down on this problem ... We must ascertain, if possible, the cause of this unrest and unhappiness; the causes of this disrespect of their neighbours' rights and laws by some of the Doukhobor people, and with its resulting terrorism and fear of injury to their fellow Christian neighbours."[17]

On 7 January 1948, after three short months, Judge Sullivan decided that he had had enough. He noted that a number of schools had been damaged by fire during the time of his appointment and concluded his inquiry by calling for "drastic action" to remedy a situation that he described as "a desperate one." He noted that to proceed further was "useless and silly" and that it was not advisable "until the crazy people are put in the mental asylum and criminals locked up in the penitentiary" (Sullivan 1948, 24).[18]

The beginning of the 1950s was a time when bombings and burnings were again on the rise and approximately 450 Sons of Freedom Doukhobors were in prison. The Royal Canadian Mounted Police (RCMP) became the new provincial police force in September 1950, replacing the former British Columbia Provincial Police. The province was entering an election year and talk about the "Doukhobor problem" was on everybody's agenda. In the spring of 1950 Attorney General Wismer requested that the president of the University of British Columbia, Norman MacKenzie, appoint a Doukhobor Research Committee that would carry out research aimed at understanding the Doukhobor situation and make recommendations for its improvement (Hawthorn 1952). Dr. Harry Hawthorn was appointed director of the research project and was the editor of the final report, in which he describes how the historical relationship between the Doukhobor groups and the government developed: "Peasant hostility to government found expression in a doctrine denying the right of governments to exist. Their sole purpose, it was held, is dominance for the purposes of exploitation, their sole basis of operations is brute force" (38).

Hawthorn goes on to describe how, over the years, the Doukhobors had adjusted to the government:

> There is still some ambivalence. Even the Sons of Freedom demand all sorts of welfare and governmental care while denying that government can serve any useful purpose and refusing the registration that could enable welfare to be given equitably. (It might be pointed out that they avoid recognizing this contradiction by the claim that they have been

cheated out of the results of their toil by the government.) The communities have long sought state protection from the arsonists, even while failing until recently to produce information against them that must have been available. (38)

The effect of the government's use of force, Hawthorn suggests, should not be underestimated. He observes that many Sons of Freedom regard prison as a virtuous place: "Instead of bringing social condemnation down on the head of the convict, punishment meted out by the government now brings social approval in its train" (Hawthorn 1952, 39). He goes on to suggest that government should devise a "specially suited system of detention for those whose psychological compulsion will force them to continue on the violent path they have been following" (ibid.).

During the time of the Doukhobor Research Committee's work, the bombing and arson continued. Geoff Andrew, from the University of British Columbia, proposed that a consultative committee be formed and that it include representatives from the Orthodox Doukhobors, the Sons of Freedom Doukhobors, and the Independent Doukhobors;[19] the provincial and federal governments; and law enforcement agencies. An unintended development was the appearance, at the first meeting of this committee, of a non-Doukhobor named Stephan Sorokin, who had arrived from Germany via the Ukraine. Mr. Sorokin was a Baptist preacher who initially appeared among the Doukhobors in Saskatchewan and then made his way to British Columbia in the spring of 1950. Immediately upon his arrival he was introduced to the Sons of Freedom community by John Lebedoff, a self-proclaimed leader (who was beginning to lose favour among the Sons of Freedom), as the long lost Doukhobor leader Peter Yastrebov. Although Stephan Sorokin denied being Peter *Yastrebov*, he was considered by many to be heaven-sent, and he remained the leader of the "Reformed" Sons of Freedom[20] until his death in 1984. The Orthodox Doukhobors, along with the Independents, saw him as an opportunist who was simply taking advantage of the Sons of Freedom. Some went so far as to suggest that he was a government "social experiment," presumably a "Pied Piper" who would lead the Sons of Freedom out of the country (Tarasoff 1982, 174).

From the minutes of the Consultative Committee on Doukhobor Affairs, it appears that the members were keen to look for any possible way to end the bombings and burnings: the key issue was the transmigration of the Sons of Freedom. According to Hawthorn's analysis, moving the Sons of Freedom, who were mainly living in Gilpin and Krestova, to a distant location was a reasonable solution to all of the problems:

This is called for in part by the fact that at Krestova and Gilpin at present there is insufficient watered land even for garden use. A place of re-settlement would need to have sources of support other than farming, and there would be some advantage for the members of the USCC and the Independents if it were distant from their localities ...

Migration or change of locality is not ordinarily an advantage in it-self in cases of social or individual problem; instead, it is often an at-tempted flight which makes a solution even more difficult of attaining. In this case, however, it is held that some move, voluntary and perhaps partial, would be justified by the ... breaking of the painful and guilty associations which their home localities now have for some Sons of Freedom. Furthermore, it is hoped that the challenge and excitement of the rebuilding and pioneering associated with a move would occupy minds and energies constructively for a time at least, giving opportu-nity for other influences to work. (Hawthorn 1952, 46-7)

Underlying this hope was the assumption that the Sons of Freedom would be willing to move to another location and that their move would bring peace to the Kootenays. Why the committee would assume this is perplexing, given that many Doukhobor people and others knew that the problems would continue until answers were found.

In June 1952 the Social Credit Party was elected in British Columbia under the leadership of W.A.C. Bennett. This government took what it saw as a no-nonsense approach to the Sons of Freedom. On 16 April 1953 Attorney General Robert Bonner announced his three-point program for solving the "Doukhobor problem": (1) those Sons of Freedom who were willing were to be permanently relocated outside of Canada; (2) those who wished to stay in Canada were to be subject to an active program of rehabilitation; and, (3) a firm attitude was to be maintained towards taxation and school attendance. Numerous places were explored for relocation, including Costa Rica, Mexico, and Adams Lake (east of Kamloops). The Sons of Freedom made it clear that they were not inter-ested in leaving the country, and although the Adams Lake area looked promising, it too eventually collapsed, as the City of Kamloops lobbied against such a move.

On 18 September 1953 Premier Bennett gave what was referred to as a policy speech in the legislature, providing a historical perspective of the Doukhobor sect and referring both to its persecution in Russia and to its early years in Canada. Premier Bennett described the numerous events that had transpired, including the previous appointment of Judge

Sullivan's commission of inquiry and the research and consultative committees. "In this entire picture I cannot, of course, take accurately into account the anxiety, inconvenience, and suffering of the people in the Kootenay Boundary area, who must live with this problem" (Bennett 1953, 5).[21] The premier went on to say that many of the recommendations in the Doukhobor Research Committee's report were being implemented, with the exception of appointing a continuing commission on Doukhobors. The premier felt that this would be best handled internally by a group of deputy ministers.

In September 1953, 148 Sons of Freedom Doukhobor adults were arrested for nudity (they were once again protesting compulsory education), leaving behind 104 children who were made wards of the superintendent of child welfare and were placed in a residential school setting in a former New Denver sanatorium. Those who were of school age, along with other Sons of Freedom children who were later apprehended by police, were required to attend school in New Denver until their parents or guardians signed an undertaking promising to send them to school. The stand-off lasted until 1959.

Prior to the children's being taken to New Denver, one of those hired by the province to assist the Consultative Committee on Doukhobor Affairs was a young educator named Hugh Herbison, who had taught some of the Sons of Freedom children during his time in Krestova. He recalled that, after the announcement was made by the attorney general regarding the government's "get tough" policy of enforced schooling, none of the children showed up again for class.[22] Finally, when he heard that the province had taken the children to New Denver, he quit his job with the consultative committee and made public his opposition to such a move.

In the early 1960s fifty-seven members of the Fraternal Council of the Christian Community and Brotherhood of Reformed Doukhobors were charged with conspiracy to intimidate the Parliament of Canada and the Legislature of British Columbia. A preliminary hearing was held in New Westminster to determine whether there was enough evidence to go to trial. The public reaction, particularly on the part of civil liberty groups, led to protests and letter-writing campaigns, the purpose of which was to get the Crown to drop the case because of the far-reaching implications such charges would have for the civil rights of dissident groups in general (Woodcock and Avakumovic 1968). The conflicting evidence presented by the Crown led Magistrate Evans to conclude that there was not sufficient evidence to proceed to trial.

During this same period another trial was held in which sixty-nine Sons of Freedom members were convicted of bombings and arson, bringing a brief end to the "reign of terror."[23] In 1962, shortly after their sentencing, the Sons of Freedom began their trek to Vancouver. The first winter they made it as far as Hope, a small town at the eastern end of the Fraser Valley, where they camped alongside the Coquihalla River. They later relocated to the Seventh Day Adventist Camp after the river overran its banks during an early spring thaw. After a few months they picked up their belongings and continued on to Vancouver, where much attention was given to their plight. Shortly after spending time in Vancouver many of them joined others who had camped outside Agassiz Mountain Prison, a new prison that had been built especially for the Sons of Freedom recently convicted of bombings. Here they spent the next ten years living in a tent village next to the prison, until the last of the Sons of Freedom were released.

All remained relatively "quiet" in the Kootenays, at least until the early 1970s when the last of the Sons of Freedom were released. Once again, fire ravaged the communities, and this led to a number of Sons of Freedom trials. The most notable occurred when the Crown charged the Orthodox Doukhobor leader John J. Verigin, along with a number of Sons of Freedom, with four counts of conspiracy to commit arson. Unlike the other indicted co-conspirators, Verigin was acquitted of two of the four charges with a stay of proceedings entered on the remaining two. Throughout the 1970s, and especially following his trial, John Verigin and other members of the Union of Spiritual Communities of Christ (USCC) made numerous attempts to get the attorney general to appoint a commission of inquiry.

In April 1979 I was hired by the Ministry of the Attorney General to prepare a report on how government might address the Doukhobor situation. Given John J. Verigin's trial and the numerous Sons of Freedom arson cases before the courts, this was a challenging time to be working for the provincial government. The credibility of the Crown was questioned not only by the Orthodox Doukhobors, who saw the trial as a "travesty," but also by the Sons of Freedom, who had testified on the Crown's behalf.

In May 1979 I submitted our report – *A Proposal for Community and Government Involvement in Doukhobor Affairs* (Herbison and Cran 1979) – to the Attorney General. In it we concluded that

at present the only mechanism government has for dealing with Doukhobor affairs is the criminal justice system. With responsibility for applying and administering the law according to due process, it cannot be expected to deal adequately with a religious-ethnic minority in all the complexity of its emotionally charged relationships. By its very terms of reference, it deals with conflict only after it erupts into illegal acts. It has no mandate to develop an improved social climate in which protest and depredation would not flourish. (2)

Meanwhile, the calls from the Orthodox Doukhobors for a commission of inquiry continued, and, shortly after the report was submitted, I was asked to develop a plan for implementing its recommendations. On 13 November 1979, at a press conference held in Cranbrook, British Columbia, the attorney general announced the formation of what became known as the Kootenay Committee on Intergroup Relations (KCIR).

Crux of the Debate

The crux of the debate both prior to and during the eight years (1979-87) of the KCIR was the Sons of Freedom claim that their mission was to save Doukhoborism. They insisted that the Orthodox leadership, in particular that of Peter Petrovich Verigin, had first nurtured them and then instructed them (albeit covertly, through the use of oblique messages), to burn and bomb, actions that they believed were essential to saving Doukhoborism.

These allegations were, for the most part, difficult to understand and accept because the Orthodox Doukhobors, particularly their leadership, had denounced bombings and arson from the very beginning and had made numerous efforts to differentiate themselves from those whom they described as "terrorists." They believed that the Sons of Freedom were using this conspiracy narrative as an excuse to confuse the public in order to elevate their own status.

The Sons of Freedom, on the other hand, have been steadfast in their beliefs and unusually strident in their actions. This has resulted, throughout most of the twentieth century, in their being publicly chastised and physically ostracized by the Orthodox Doukhobors and their leaders. Their persistence in pursuing the "truth" leaves one to ask what they expected to gain from their efforts and their many spent years in prison, on hunger fasts, while sacrificing their health and families for "the cause."

There was another group, known as the "Reformed Doukhobors"[24] or "Reformed Sons of Freedom," which was started by Stephan Sorokin soon after his arrival in 1950. The Reformed Doukhobors represented Sons of Freedom who were no longer interested in going to jail for the "cause." Many had already spent time in prison, with some having lost their health or their loved ones. All were resentful of the Orthodox leadership, whom they believed was responsible for disrupting their lives. Their actions were no less strident than were those of the Sons of Freedom. They published their own communiqués, which they circulated far and wide and in which they accused different people, be they Orthodox or Independent, of conspiring with the Sons of Freedom and/or taunting them to burn or bomb, all of which they saw as cultural hypocrisy in the name of Doukhoborism. Although he was not always present as he spent a considerable amount of time in Montevideo, Uruguay, Stephan Sorokin at times seemed to smooth the rough edges of the debate; however, at other times he seemed to do the opposite, as, for example, when he saw the Soviets becoming more active, throughout the 1970s, with the Orthodox leadership.

The Orthodox members were caught in this vitriolic cultural tangle. They methodically rebuilt their community centres, which had been destroyed not once but many times over the years, and they spent part of their livelihood guarding not only their own properties but also the Verigin residences, the community centres, and other community property.

The non-Doukhobor public, especially those living in the Kootenay and Boundary region, never knew what to make of the idiosyncratic nature of the Doukhobor people. This was not an easy time for them either as their lives were disrupted by, among other things, police roadblocks; people protesting in the nude; blazing buildings; twisted rail; destroyed bridges; a dynamited transmission pole that trapped 200 miners; and reports of dynamite found under an Anglican Church, on a BC ferry, and in bus stations. This left the weary members of the public demanding that either the provincial government do something or they would do something themselves. As time went on, the pitch of desperation reached the level of a scream.

2
Deconstructing the Discourse of Conflict and Culture

Trying to make sense of what happened over the many years that the Doukhobors had been in Canada left me wondering where to begin. How did bread, water, and salt mix with nitroglycerin and ammonium nitrate? What do the Doukhobors mean when they say "know the truth and truth shall set you free"? Whose truth? These were the questions that haunted me and kept me awake off and on throughout those first nine years. And now that twenty years has passed, the nocturnal question has become: what happened that enabled the turmoil to end?

My quest as a doctoral student involved returning to my developmental years as a young bureaucrat; reviewing old files (which I still kept in my office) that contained correspondence, reports, and photographs; and looking at published articles, theses, and over 100 transcripts from the Expanded Kootenay Committee on Intergroup Relations (EKCIR)[1] sessions, which were held between 1982 and 1987. Rereading the transcripts helped me to recall the stories that had guided the sessions. But it also helped me to identify the particular narratives that shaped the events occurring at the time. To piece together my own stories I had my journals, which functioned as a startling reminder of how consuming the provincial government's assignment had been during that period of my life.

Rendering the Past
Reviewing the literature was reasonably straightforward; however, the thought of returning to the Kootenays to revisit some of the sights and to interview those who had played a key role during the 1980s gave me pause. Would those whom I knew as a government representative view me differently in my new role as a graduate student? Would they be willing to share their perceptions of conflict and the views they held of

others, including me, at the time? I viewed myself as integral to the conflict not only because of my previous assignment but also because I know I cannot simply detach myself from my own history, biases, and beliefs. I was cognizant of the need to maintain a balance between their stories and my perceptions, their meanings and my meanings, their biases and mine. Would we be able to have the sort of conversation in which we could openly discuss the undiscussed and examine what was once merely polemic?

I decided to limit my interviews to those who played a crucial role both during the EKCIR sessions and when we established a research committee to examine the 1924 Canadian Pacific Railway (CPR) train explosion.[2] I interviewed Jim Popoff from the USCC. Popoff, whose father was a noted Doukhobor historian, was a key spokesperson for the Orthodox Doukhobors during the EKCIR and was a former editor of *Iskra* and Mir Publications. I also interviewed Fred Makortoff and Steve Lapshinoff, both of whom grew up in Sons of Freedom families in different parts of the Kootenay and Boundary regions, and both of whom later joined the Fraternal Council of the Christian Community and Brotherhood of Reformed Doukhobors under Stephan Sorokin's leadership. Steve Lapshinoff was a key researcher both for the Reformed Doukhobors and later for the EKCIR; Fred Makortoff was a spokesman for the Reformed Doukhobors and a translator of and confidante to Stephan Sorokin.

I began by asking the interviewees, each of whom lived in a different location in different circumstances, to describe what it was like growing up in their respective communities. I was curious to know what they remembered from their youth and was especially eager to hear the stories they told about other groups. I also asked them about the "turning points," or "epiphanies," that emerged during the EKCIR sessions – events that not only illuminated their thinking but that also challenged their assumptions, views, and judgments.[3] And I wanted to know how they viewed the situation now, after the passage of nearly twenty years.

My first interview was with Steve Lapshinoff and it took place on 15 November 2001 at his home in Krestova, where he lives with Ann Sorokin, Stephan Sorokin's former wife. As I drove up to their place I remembered my first visit back in the late spring of 1979. Mr. Sorokin's place was a compound-like structure, with guards situated at the entrance to the property. This time as I entered the property there were neither guards nor a gate but, rather, a lawn and gardens.

I parked my car between the house and the small wooden building where I first met Stephan Sorokin, along with Fred Makortoff, Steve Lapshinoff, and other members of the Fraternal Council. The current

Sorokin house was a modular home-type structure that had been built in the mid-1970s, after the former Sorokin house had been set ablaze. Ann Sorokin's and Steve Lapshinoff's home was orderly and hospitable.

That evening I met with Jim Popoff at the motel where I was staying in Grand Forks. The room was made of cinder blocks, typical of motels built back in the 1980s, and I found it to be rather cold and Spartan. Situated between us was a small, wobbly table that held my tape recorder and my list of questions. My conversations that day with both Mr. Lapshinoff and Mr. Popoff were candid and insightful.

The evening of the following day I met with Fred Makortoff at his home in South Slocan (overlooking Bonnington Falls on the Kootenay River), where he lives with his wife Elizaveta and her father. The Makortoff home was warm and inviting, a sharp contrast to the cinder block space I visited the night before.

The interviews ranged from four to eight hours. My plan was to follow them up by having all three interviewees participate in a discussion that I would facilitate, its purpose being to explore any differences with regard to recalling past events. However, after reviewing the transcripts I realized that the interviewees' recollections of events contained only minor differences. So, rather than organize a joint interview, I asked each person to comment on my rendering of their stories (and, later, on the chapters of this book).

Searching for Theories and Underlying Assumptions

After returning home I began to piece together theories about culture and conflict and waded through numerous academic studies on the Doukhobors. The conflict theories were drawn from a range of disciplines, most notably psychology, sociology, and anthropology, and were based on a set of premises that had been derived from linear thinking. Some of these theories are now fundamental to the conflict resolution field. However, my years of experience had taught me that reducing conflict narratives to "issues" to be "resolved" did not work in situations that involved multilayered, complex stories and myths drawn from both oral traditions and modern-day discourse. This is not to suggest that the Doukhobor people did not have "issues": there were plenty of issues. However, what was fundamental to these people and their context were competing narratives and patterns of communication that had been intricately shaped throughout 400 years of culture making. What I learned was that any attempt to reduce their stories and opinions into chunks of resolvable issues turned discussions into what one might describe as chaotic episodes of visceral theatrics.

Notion of Truth

There have been numerous articles, books, and theses written about the Doukhobors. Some are written by Doukhobors, and these include Peter N. Maloff (1950, 1957); Simeon Reibin (1971); Koozma Tarasoff (1963, 1969, 1982); and Eli Popoff (1992). Others are written by non-Doukhobors, and these include Maude (1904); Bonch-Bruevich (1909); Reid (1932); Wright (1940); Hirabayashi (1951); Zubek and Solberg (1952); Franz (1958); Holt (1964); Bockemuehl(1968); Woodcock and Avakumovic (1968); Dunn (1970); Mealing (1975); and McLaren (1995a, 1995b), to name a few. The most comprehensive study of the Doukhobors is *The Doukhobors of British Columbia*, a report conducted by the Doukhobor Research Committee in the early 1950s and edited by Harry Hawthorn (1952). It covers a wide range of subjects related to the Doukhobors, from agricultural practices to psychoanalytic analyses of the Sons of Freedom. All of these materials have contributed in some way to the acknowledgment of the differences between the Sons of Freedom and other Doukhobors and to the conclusion that acts of destruction are the sole responsibility of the former.

In reviewing the Doukhobor literature I began with the first book written about the Doukhobors soon after their arrival in Canada in 1899. Aylmer Maude, along with Prince D.A. Hilkoff and two Doukhobor families, came to Canada in 1898 to begin negotiating the terms for bringing the sect to this country as, at that time, the Canadian government was keen to attract new immigrants. Maude chronicled his experience in *A Peculiar People: The Doukhobors*, which was published in 1904. He depicted the Doukhobors as, for the most part,

> an illiterate folk, who seldom put their thoughts on paper. They accepted the decisions of recognized Leaders, one of whom always came into authority as soon as his predecessor died. Through long years of persecution they learnt to conceal their beliefs; and it is impossible to say with certainty and exactitude what, as a community, they have believed at any given moment, though the main trend of their thought, and the matters of practice on which they differed from their neighbours are plainly discernible. (5)

Their distinguishing cultural trait, Maude tells us, is obstinacy. This obstinacy may be seen in their defence of their own doctrine as well as in their attacks on those who differ from them. Each Doukhobor listens to his or her own internal voice as well as to the voices of others, especially that of the leadership. Such voices, Maude suggests, are often manifested in some kind of symbolic form or special code, such as wearing the colour red or referring to dynamite as "fruit."

There are numerous contradictory statements concerning what various spiritual leaders meant. For instance, what a leader or his close associate says publicly may not be consistent with what is said to certain members in private conversations. For example, Maude notes that, back in 1902, in his public pronouncements Peter V. Verigin advocated compliance with Canadian laws; however, many Doukhobors believed that he was merely doing this to protect himself, while, in fact, he wanted people to continue their resistance. For Aylmer Maude, the Doukhobor notion of "truth" was a cultural encumbrance that made his role as an intermediary between the Doukhobors and the government difficult at best. This is evidenced by numerous misunderstandings that arose over land purchases in Saskatchewan.

Charles Franz (1958, 98), who arrived on the scene considerably later than Maude, seems to agree with him when, in his dissertation, he comments: "all Doukhobors received sanctioned approval for prevarication." He notes that there were numerous testimonials and confessions presented to royal commissions and criminal court proceedings, and he concludes that "the validity of these statements ... generally has been vitiated by the practice of widespread deceit and falsification toward outsiders" (ibid.). Franz also notes that, with regard to Doukhobor relations with government personnel, the Doukhobor's "secret, deceptive, and aggressive practices have been most highly developed." Some of these practices were in the form of nude parades, burnings, and bombings, while some in the form of attempting to strip government officials.[4]

Franz no doubt recognizes the challenge that these types of behaviour present to social science fieldwork as a whole: how does one discern fact from fiction? What is "truth"? How might truth be characterized by those who claim to know "it"? And what, or whose, purpose is served by those who search for truth?

For Franz (1958), "truth" was lost in the cultural and historical landscape in which the Doukhobors lived. Their inconsistent truth claims became a methodological issue for him as well as for other anthropologists whose search for cultural authenticity was a primary aim. As Bruner (1990) asserts, maintaining methodological integrity is an ongoing problem in science as the logic of science structures the nature of the outcome, which, in turn, limits the reliability of the information. My approach to the Doukhobor situation was to search not for the truth but, rather, to examine the reasons their stories were told. What were the underlying constructions of meaning from which the narrators drew? How did these stories and meanings influence the way people perceived situations and each other?

Mining for a Paradigm

There is no question that, from a modernist perspective, science involves the pursuit of "truth," which stands in contrast to the postmodernist perspective, which involves seeing "truth," regardless of its standing in science, as a social construction rather than as a discovery. This is not to raise the relativist argument, which ends up in the quagmire of every belief being as good as every other, but, rather, to posit that "truths" are human constructions, that they are not invincible, and that they can often differ. Here, the emphasis is on the meanings constructed from narratives that, when applied to a conflict setting, not only contextualize the conflict but, conceivably, aid in furthering understanding. This stands in sharp contrast to the fact-finding approach to conflict resolution, which sets out to prove who is right and who is wrong; it also stands in sharp contrast to the positivist approach, which posits the existence of a singular truth.

Maude (1904) and Franz (1958), as well as others, failed to determine what might have been the underlying reasons the Doukhobors appeared to be "obstinate," "deceitful," and "prevaricators of the truth"; or why some truth claims remained dominant while others were discounted or marginalized. This led me to realize that I needed to look at the narratives themselves. This meant focusing on the story as told rather than on the logic and alleged "facts" so dear to the modernist approach.

I recognize that this is a departure for those who conceive of narratives as "literature," or for those who view narratives simply as anecdotes (such as lawyers, who use anecdotal evidence to appeal to emotion rather than logic). In science, anecdotes are thought of as "soft science," and anecdotal evidence, when used to describe a given argument or as a method of data collection, is viewed disparagingly. However, as Lyotard (1984, xxiii) would attest, "science has always been in conflict with narratives," without recognizing its own duplicity. For instance, if the role of the researcher were to be examined, we would see that the research report is, in fact, the researcher's own narrative – a narrative that contains not only a theoretical framework, analysis, findings, and conclusions but also the researcher's worldview, cultural assumptions, biases, and beliefs.

I came across a report by Alfred Shulman (1952), a psychiatrist from the Seton Institute in Baltimore, who was a member of Hawthorn's research committee. In his report, *The Personality Characteristics and Psychological Problems of the Doukhobors,* Shulman explains the difficulties that the Doukhobors had in relating with one another as well as with the non-Doukhobor population. He talked about how he applied three different techniques to his examination of the Doukhobors: (1) life histories, (2) psychiatric interviews, and (3) projective tests. He said that his tests (Rorschach and Murray's Thematic Apperception Test) were of little value because the suspiciousness of the informants prevented him from administering them. Although he did find the psychiatric interviews to be "profitable," the methods he used to elicit an individual's life history were not. He reports that "it was rarely possible to find an informant sufficiently accurate, honest and fluent to talk about himself in a meaningful way" (138). He found that many of the Doukhobor people he interviewed would "leap blindly to any interpretation that does the faintest of justice to the facts, and cling with a tenacious disregard for reality" (144). Rather than focusing on the reasons that this might have been the case, Shulmann concluded that this type of thinking was a form of "autism," which he suggested created considerable problems in the way people communicate with each other: "Their autism radically interferes with a realistic appraisal of any situation and allows them to substitute naive wishful thinking" (144).

Shulman's narrative tells us more about his own assumptions and meaning constructions as a psychiatrist than it does about the nature of the Doukhobor conflict. His rendering of their actions is filtered through the lens of his profession, which gives his role a sense of legitimacy and authenticity. Counter to this view, Thomas Szasz (1970) would argue that "mental illness" or "social pathology" (or, for that matter, "autism") are no more than labels conferred on those individuals who are "different"; that is, who do not conform to society's definitions of appropriate behaviour. Unfortunately, Shulman's social psychoanalysis does not speak to the reasons why certain people choose to be different (or, for that matter, why all people are expected to be the same).

Another set of unexamined assumptions may be seen in a paper presented by Dr. William Plenderleith, coordinator of special services for the British Columbia Department of Education. He was involved in the decision making that led to the removal of the Sons of Freedom children from their homes in 1953. After the children were released from New Denver, Plenderleith recommended that the former superintendent of the New Denver Dormitory, John Clarkson, be awarded for his public service achievement.[5] In his remarks he gratuitously "psycho-analyzed" the Sons of Freedom as though they, like, Clarkson, constituted a single being.

> the Freedomites have had the ... frustrating experience of being ostracised from their parent body. This ostracization became an important factor in influencing the Freedomites' attitude toward society. They no longer "belonged" to the parent group. They no longer shared any communal property. They were outcasts, squatting on government-owned land. They were social failures, totally unable to cope with the problem of life in Canada.[6]

What Plenderleith failed to recognize was that all Doukhobors, not just the Sons of Freedom, were, as he describes it, "squatting on government property" due to the collapse of the Christian Community of Universal Brotherhood (CCUB Ltd.) in 1939. Moreover, all of the Doukhobors, including the Sons of Freedom, continued to occupy their former lands, which were held by the Crown from 1939 to 1965 and then sold back to the Doukhobor occupants.

Plenderleith extended his "illness metaphor" to describe how the Sons of Freedom needed to compensate for their feelings of inferiority by making themselves "martyrs to a cause." He asserted that they professed to care nothing for material wealth and "let their houses fall into a state of disrepair" because they "craved public recognition of the self-sacrificing par."[7] Again what Plenderleith fails to recognize is that none of the Doukhobor or Sons of Freedom houses had finished exteriors; however, the interiors were always impeccably clean and orderly. This is something he would have known if he had bothered to ask, never mind actually to visit those about whom he wrote so freely.

Both Shulman's and Plenderleith's stories were given a certain prominence because of the positions their authors held. Shulman's, in particular, appears to have influenced the BC government to consider ending the cycle of destruction by directing its efforts towards the children rather than their parents, who, given the autism diagnosis, were no longer considered "curable."

Lyotard (1984) suggests that the grand theories (or "metanarratives," as he calls them) that Shulman and Plenderleith relied upon were in decline. In applying a narrative approach to conflict situations, one considers the people's stories and their "social, moral and political consequences ... and their situational impact" (Seidman 1995, 17). This is not to say that the narrative approach is the saviour of social science but simply to suggest that, in conflict situations, there is often a need to examine both the text and subtext of the story structure.[8]

Use of Narratives

A narrative is a representation of an event that we abstract from our own experience or from the experience of others. The use of narratives is well established. Anthropologists like Victor Turner (1980), for example, use narratives to "formulate the processional form" of "social dramas."[9] These dramas are expressive "episodes" in which certain community conflicts are acted out and resolved. This may take the shape of a shaming feast among an indigenous tribe, the confessional within the Roman Catholic Church, or a court of law in British Columbia. Turner argues that the narratives of those featured in such social dramas provide the community with a variety of potential paths to conciliation, reconciliation, or to simply gaining social recognition.

Paul Ricoeur (1970, 1997) views narratives as structures that undergird the process of identity formation. Michael White and David Epston (1990, 27) further suggest that we organize and give meaning to who we are through what they term the "storying of our experience." The Doukhobors have 400 years of history that has helped shape how they view themselves and how they wish others to view them. Their stories are the receptacle of their values and beliefs, which they have passed orally from generation to generation. The Sons of Freedom would argue that they were defending these values and beliefs and that of course they used these stories to justify their actions. The storying of experience adds an existential dimension to the notion of narrative, and underscoring this dimension are the meanings that serve as the cultural framework that defines each group.

John Winslade and Gerald Monk (2000) mix narrative psychology with conflict resolution discourse to create a hybrid form of mediation practice that uses techniques such as discursive listening to unlock the cultural discourses underpinning one's story. They claim that, through enabling self-realization, this process liberates an individual's sense of self from the interlocking tangles of a given dispute. The narrative approach to conflict is our way of being in the world. And, in the telling of stories, we create order and chaos, stability and instability, as well as meaning and ambiguity. In other words, narratives satisfy our impulse to share our experiences, understandings, and meanings as well as to convey our needs, fears, and dreams. For some, however, the notion of narrative may seem unruly and irreverent, and many may ask: How can one be in the world without knowing truth?

My assertion is that truth is a social construction that presupposes the presence of fact. As adaptive cultural beings we often take it for granted that people modify their behaviour and render their accounts so as to enable them to adapt to the setting within which they find themselves. "People are expected to behave situationally whatever their 'roles,' whether they are introverted or extroverted, whatever their scores on the Minnesota Multiphasic Personality Inventory (MMPI), whatever their politics" (Bruner 1990, 48). But they also behave situationally in choosing how and to whom certain stories are told. How one behaves in a boardroom, for example, is different from how one behaves in a restaurant or at a sports event. We apply logic and discretion when it comes to choosing how we tell a story, and we modify the narration to adapt to the setting in which the story is told. Thus the notion of truth is relative to the purpose served by the story.

Narrative Structure

Linear thinking, generalization, and objectification are common practices in Western culture, and they influence how we think and act. Certain structures and rules shape and form our discourse;[10] without these structures and rules dissonance emerges. How we deal with this dissonance is also situational. For instance, we are more likely to tolerate "incoherence" from someone who is infirm than we are from someone who is not. We expect a story to be presented in a logical way. We also expect that, if the story is a rendering of someone's past, then it should be true and factual.

Bruner (1990) describes this Western approach to life as "paradigmatic." We use "facts" to verify "truth," whether in scientific or legal discourse. He suggests that an alternative to this approach involves an emphasis on what he terms "meaningfulness," whereby narratives no longer need to verify "truth" but, rather, need merely to feature the verisimilitude of the story. In other words, it is the story line that is the focus rather than the "facts." These are narratives of meaning, and they are situated within an individual's experience of a place or event rather than in abstract thoughts or ideas. Narratives are not intended to diminish what one conceives of as "truthfulness" but, rather, to show how meaning is constructed and negotiated during interactions with others.

A narrative relies on the relationship between "storying" and sense-making. Stories require a structure and organization that gives a coherence and symmetry to their rendering. But stories also require an event, because without an event one would be left with a description, a lyric, or an argument – all of which, in terms of sense making, rely on a different set of structures than do stories.

Like stories, language has its own set of rules and conventions that enables it to be studied. However, as David Abram (1996, 84) suggests, at the heart of language "is the poetic productivity of expressive speech." The Sons of Freedom exemplified this "poetic productivity" in the myriad number of signs and codes (e.g., "red" to signify fire or "fruit" to signify dynamite) and mannerisms (e.g., nudity) through which they communicated. This meant that one had to be part of the community of discourse in order to understand the nuances of what was said. Often, individuals would destroy their own or another's property on the basis of someone's dream. This is where facts become irrelevant and truth notional.

Discourse of Culture

Culture is a ubiquitous term. What do we need to know about culture to understand the nature of conflict? Or, conversely, what do we need to know about conflict to understand the nature of culture? Brannan, Esler, and Strindberg (2001, 15) define culture as "sets of behaviours that are fairly predictable" and are "capable of being presented in generalized and typical patterns." This suggests that the members of each culture operate in accordance with a set of social norms and that this enables them to interact with one other in different settings.

There are numerous cultural theorists, but Geert Hofstede (1980) was noted for his work on the dimensions of culture exemplified through his use of the notions of "individualist" and "collectivist," which he applied to different nationalities. For example, in a collectivist setting one might find a set of values, commitments, and identifications that are held in common among group members; whereas, in an individualist setting (like those in the West), values, commitments, and identifications are more variable, with group membership being more fluid and less confined to specific set of values than is the case in collectivist settings. In Hofstede's view, the Doukhobors are homogeneous and their collective interests are commonly held among members. This may be true for some of the early Doukhobor settlers who lived in a village, or *Mir,* system; however, once they set foot on Canadian soil, Doukhobor members began to leave the villages to become Independents (Tarasoff 1963). For these people, Hofstede's model does not apply.

Although Hofstede's reductionist approach to culture remains popular, Avruch, Black, and Scimecca (1991) offer a more relational view of culture. They see individual cultural experience as being mediated by perceptions and meanings, which they view as socially constructed and as differing from family to family, group to group, and nation to nation. They also noted a number of misconceptions regarding how culture is viewed, and they noted that each of these had implications for addressing conflict. These misconceptions include seeing culture as a thing (which Avruch, Black, and Scimecca view as the objectification of culture rather than as a property of human consciousness) and seeing culture as "uniformly distributed across a group" (which presumes that everyone is the same or at least maintains a certain historical group identity).

To objectify culture is to ignore individual behaviour, and a uniform-distribution view of culture stereotypes behaviour. When culture is viewed as an object or as a category of sameness (whether collectivist or individualist), the solution to conflict is viewed in a similarly metaphorical way. For example, if culture is viewed as an elaborate machine, then we are inclined to view conflict as a breakdown of that machine and to view the repairing of that breakdown as the appropriate fix. If, on the other hand, we view culture as an organism, then conflict is viewed as a disease and the appropriate solution involves identifying the pathology and applying the correct diagnosis (White and Epston 1990). Both of these metaphoric approaches to conflict become problematic by virtue of their totalizing effect, regardless of whether conflict arises within or between cultures. If we conceptualize conflict using a particular metaphor, then the metaphor shapes our view of the "solution," which, depending on the metaphor, narrows the options for addressing the conflict.

One alternative to the above approaches to conflict is a multicultural approach that holds that, in dealing with people who are different, it is appropriate to "get to know their culture." Getting to know another's culture has been a particularly popular goal for governments; however, it has created a rather impoverished conception of culture, rendering it synonymous with what you cook or wear. It results in one's comparing differences between cultures rather than learning about similarities. Furthermore, knowledge about other cultures does not necessarily address the problem of ethnocentrism, or of ideological positions that may affect certain ethnic groups more than others.

Avruch, Black, and Scimecca (1991) use a "culture-as-consciousness" approach to conflict, which assumes that there is a plurality of views within any identifiable group, whether that group is perceived as ethnic or religious or whatever. This approach enables one to ask: "How is conflict conceptualized among [the group's] members or by the parties [to the dispute]? What meaning does an event so construed have? What normative weight is given to situations of conflict?" (31). These are questions that do not assume uniformity but, rather, recognize that groups contain individuals who may share constructed meanings pertaining to events experienced in common. I prefer to use the "culture-as-consciousness" approach to conflict as it challenges taken-for-granted assumptions about culture and conflict; that is, it does not assume there can be a one-solution-fits-all outcome.

Discourse of Conflict

The word "conflict" is derived from Middle English, from the Latin *conflictus* (an act of striking together) as well as from the French *confligere* (to strike together). Conflict theorists like Tjosvold (1991) suggest that conflicts have traditionally been defined as opposing interests that involve scarce resources, goal divergence, and frustration. Folger, Poole, and Stutman (1996) view conflict as the interaction of interdependent people who have incompatible goals and who interfere with each other in their attempts to achieve them. And Pruitt, Rubin, and Kim (1994) argue that conflict is a perceived divergence of interest resulting in the belief that the aspirations of the parties to the dispute cannot simultaneously be achieved. These conceptions of conflict use an economic metaphor involving scarcity of resources and/or competition, resulting in incompatible goals and/or a struggle over value and truth claims.[11] This all seems rather self-serving and individualistic. Do the same conflict metaphors work when dissimilar groups share similar principles and beliefs or vice versa? Simmel (1955) and Coser (1956) argue that conflict, albeit self-serving for some, is important as it can create and maintain unity within or among groups whenever they deal with enmity or reciprocal antagonism.

Conflict Theories

The interdisciplinary field of conflict studies is laden with modernist notions. Examples of such notions include frustration-aggression, social identity, self-categorization, and human need theories. This is not to suggest that other theories, such as economic determinism, structural functionalism, and those related to power and deviance have not been considered: they have. The significance, however, of focusing on frustration-aggression, social identity, self-categorization, and human need theories is that they have an inordinate influence within conflict resolution literature. My purpose in presenting these theories is to demonstrate their limitations when they are applied to the Doukhobor situation.

Frustration-Aggression Theory

Dollard, Doob, Miller, Mowrer, and Sears (1939) posited that aggressive behaviour always presupposes the existence of frustration. Gilula and Daniels (1969) later argued that, although aggression originates in frustration, it comes to the fore when an individual's ongoing purposeful activity is interfered with. In other words, a person feels frustrated when his or her hopes or expectations are violated.

When frustration emerges it is acted out in various forms, ranging from personal insults or threats to the thwarting of basic needs to relative deprivation. In all cases there is a discrepancy between one's value expectations and the capacity of one's environment to satisfy those expectations. Dollard et al. (1939) viewed this as learned behaviour and held that, in order to reduce this type of response, one needed to address the factors that caused the frustration. The difficulty with this theory is that it does not address the possibility that aggressive acts may be the result of factors that have little to do with frustration. Also, frustration may have little to do with other people but may, in fact, arise from one's own inadequacy or some kind of self-limiting expectation.

Social Identity Theory

Another important development in the field of conflict studies involves the creation of social identity theories, which were introduced by Henri Tajfel (1978) in the late 1970s and again later, with John Turner (1986). Social identity theory emphasizes the significance of the subject's social situation. It categorizes, identifies, and compares objects and people by assigning certain identities to help explain their comparative relationships with each other and with their environment. For example, we categorize objects by assigning them a certain meaning, much as science categorizes people by assigning them a race, an ethnicity, a class, or a religion.

Of course, categorizing people into assigned identities is the mainstay of certain professions, psychology being a primary example. Shulman (1952, 166) described the Sons of Freedom group as "those who fit nowhere else." He argued that five types of individuals were likely to join the Sons of Freedom: (1) individuals who were aggressively bent and who had failed to satisfy their needs, either as a USCC (Orthodox) member or as an Independent; (2) individuals who were passive, lonely, or guilty men who submerged themselves in the formless mass of the Sons of Freedom in order to atone for their wrongdoings; (3) individuals who were pathological and who would not be tolerated in any society; (4)

individuals who were old and who lacked both special training and self-esteem; and (5) individuals who were emotionally impoverished and constricted. Shulman's types were based on a medical model. In her *Therapeutic Process as the Social Construction of Change*,[12] Laura Fruggeri (1992) suggests that when you switch from the medical model to a different paradigm (such as that offered by social constructionism), then the medical model – upon which psychotherapy relies – can be demystified. And, with this demystification, the psychoanalytic narrative can transform into a different kind of narrative.

How are identities chosen? What purpose do they serve in helping to explain conflict? There are those who are able to shape their own identities in accord with whom they wish to associate, but there are also those whose identities are assigned to them by others, on the basis of skin colour, gender, age, size, or class. These categories are not chosen by the individuals in question but, rather, are assigned in order to differentiate one group from another. As we see in Shulman's analysis, with these assigned categories come "labels."[13] The Doukhobors were labelled through images constructed in the media. The Orthodox Doukhobors took measures to ensure a clear separation between themselves and the Sons of Freedom. For the Sons of Freedom this meant having to reconcile two conflicting identities – how they saw themselves (spiritualists) and how others saw them (terrorists).

Self-Categorization Theory

John Turner, along with his colleagues Hogg, Oakes, Reicher, and Wetherell (1987), reconceptualized social identity theory, transforming it into what they called self-categorization theory. This theory is used to categorize an individual's self-concept. It postulates that, at different times, an individual perceives him- or herself to be unique and at other times to be part of a group. Both are equally valid expressions of self. The extent to which we define ourselves at either the personal or the social level can be both fluid and functionally antagonistic. For instance, a conflict between self-interest at the personal level and self-interest at the group level results in our perceiving ourselves as less unique than might have been the case had a conflict not occurred. This may help to explain the relationship between self and others in a "Western" sense, but it does not take into account the cultural context of the individual in relation to his or her family, caste, or other social variables.

Social identity and self-categorization theories led to the development, in the 1970s and 1980s, of a generic theory of human behaviour known as human needs theory.

Human Needs Theory

John Burton (1990) has often been credited with the development of human needs theory as it relates to the field of conflict resolution. Burton's theory, which has been characterized as a cluster of identity needs, examines how individual and group identity are formed and how environment (natural and social) influences human development. Human needs theory is based on the belief that each individual has basic needs that must be met if we are to maintain stable societies.[14]

Burton proposed a cluster of nine basic human needs:

1 Consistency in response (learning and behaviour)
2 Stimulation (awakens in the individual the desire to learn)
3 Security (without security the individual will withdraw and will not learn or contribute)
4 Recognition (individual's need for confirmation, approval and encouragement for seeking identity)
5 Distributive justice (appropriate response or reward)
6 Development and appearance of rationality (acting consistently and expecting consistency from others)
7 Meaningful responses (sincerity with others)
8 Sense of control (self-defense)
9 Defense of one's role (role preservation).

Human needs theory makes some bold assumptions. For instance, it assumes that the causes of human behaviour are socio-biological rather than cultural and that certain human needs are essential to human development and social stability. The presumption is that culture may be reduced to an "overlay" superimposed on biologically determined human nature. This socio-biological approach to understanding conflict does not take into account the cultural side of the debate. For example, Bruner (1990, 21) would argue that biology does not cause humans to act but, rather, serves as "a constraint upon [action] or a condition for it": "the engine in the car does not 'cause' us to drive to the supermarket for the week's shopping." I raise this point not to fuel the old "nurture-versus-nature" debate but, rather, as a reminder that whatever position one adopts it carries within it culturally embedded a priori assumptions that need to be acknowledged.

Summarizing the Discourses

From the literature it is clear that, when we objectify conflict, we create a uniform-distribution view that ignores culture and context and that presumes that conflict is resolvable through the application of process-directed models. What is assumed is that *all* conflicts occur because someone's needs are not being met or someone's goals are being threatened. This suggests that individuals are internally driven, with each pursuing a path of self-interest. This approach does not take into account the possibility that conflict might be used to serve other purposes. There are more functional interpretations of conflict, such as that of Simmel (1955), who suggested that enmities and reciprocal antagonisms are important in maintaining a balance between groups. Like Simmel, Lewis Coser (1956) posited that conflict within a group may help to establish or re-establish unity and cohesion where it has been threatened by hostile and antagonistic feelings among members.[15]

In his article, "Sons of Freedom and the Canadian State," which appeared in *Canadian Ethnic Studies* in 1984, Colin Yerbury furthers Coser's argument by describing the Sons of Freedom as a "revivalist subsect," who

> generally place the onus of their problems and distress back onto their individual members: disciples are urged to adopt a pure life without smoking, drinking, lying, fornication and so forth in order to attain new identity, free from sin and ready for the promise of eternal life. Extremist revitalization processes involve purification rituals of burning material possessions. Such actions serve as a mechanism for temporarily increasing group unity. (Yerbury 1984, 49)

Disappointingly, Yerbury gives us no indication of how he came to this view or, for that matter, how he arrived at his conclusion that the reason for the conflict's continuing concerns the government's "political opportunism and the unfounded fear of an organized terrorist conspiracy." This he describes as "the prime reasons for the enactment of retrograde legislation at a time when government may have found it advantageous not to interfere with revitalization processes" (66). Unfortunately, his "analysis" is rather impoverished, given that there is no evidence that he has had any involvement whatsoever with those about whom he writes. This, in itself, is a form of labelling, and it is based upon the assumptions, the ill-conceived conclusions, and the cultural and personal biases of the writers and newspaper editorialists upon whom Yerbury has chosen to rely.

In reviewing the literature it became evident to me that current conflict theories are unacceptably reductionist. If we were to view the conflict situation as stemming from frustration, as a human need, or as having to do with social identity, then we may be able to explain certain elements of the conflict setting. However, I contend that this would be a fractured representation, deficient with regard both to context and to interrelatedness.

Each conflict theory arises from within its own field, be it psychology, sociology, or subsets thereof, and, in so doing, it decontextualizes the connections between the varying parts. For example, how do we come to understand the behaviour we are observing without knowing something about the individual, the structural conditions within the environment, and the cultural influences that are brought to bear at the observable moment of intersection? Explanations are easy to come by, whether they are informed through theory or through some other means. The challenge is to deconstruct the moment of observation by taking into account not only that which is being observed but also the observer. For without knowing what assumptions are being made, how can we draw reasonable conclusions?

There is more to understanding conflict than explaining conflict situations through theory. The theories currently being used to explain the nature of conflict, like the reductionist processes and methodologies from which they sprang, provide a reductionist understanding of conflict. As a result, we come to view conflict intervention in the same reductionist way: we deem entities and issues to be "resolvable" and then wonder why all conflict situations cannot be "resolved" in the same manner.

Because I am guided by trying to determine the contributing factors that brought an end to the bombings and arson, I find myself focusing on the narratives and the storytelling experience in order to learn more about (1) how certain competing narratives metastasized into conflict, (2) the purpose served by the telling of these stories, and (3) what factors led to change. This requires an approach to conflict that assumes that people organize their experiences though stories in order to make sense of their lives and their relationships with others. It also assumes that, through the retelling of stories, people not only mythologize those elements that shape identity but also self-organize into communities of discourse.

3
Auto-Narrative

My interest in narratives began while I was working with the Doukhobor communities back in the late 1970s and early 1980s as the attorney general's liaison for Doukhobor affairs. When I first began my assignment certain stories were shrouded in secrecy, while others were like quiet screams for help. I listened to individuals tell their stories about events that had occurred many decades before, in detail and with seeming precision. Some would recall the words of a former leader at a specific gathering that had occurred forty or fifty years previously as though they had heard the words that morning. Although I marvelled at this ability, a certain dissonance emerged when I thought about how these same stories had contained symbolic messages that led to fire, bombings, and nude protests.

Getting Started

It was 18 March 1979 when I met with Mark Krasnick in Vancouver at what was then the new Arthur Erickson-designed law court. Mark was the assistant deputy minister for policy planning for the BC Attorney General's Office. I was twenty-eight years old and had been working for the Ministry of the Attorney General on a short-term basis, organizing justice councils throughout the Kootenay region.[1]

Mark asked if I would prepare a report for the attorney general that would describe how the "Doukhobor problem" might be addressed differently from how it had been. Up until then the Doukhobor situation had been considered a policing operation; however, for some reason the Ministry of the Attorney General was looking for a new approach to the conflict. I wasn't sure exactly what I would do, but I couldn't think of any reason why I should decline his request. I was young, naïve, and confident that I was capable of solving anything. My only request was that I be allowed to hire Hugh Herbison to assist in researching and writing the report. Hugh was a retired educator living in the Quaker community of Argenta, and he had worked with the Sons of Freedom Doukhobor community during the late 1940s and early 1950s.

It took me no time at all to realize that this was not a good time to be representing the provincial government in the Kootenays, where most of the Doukhobors were located. There were numerous Sons of Freedom arson cases before the courts. In one such case the leader of the Orthodox group, John J. Verigin, was charged with four counts of conspiracy to commit arson, and this had left the Orthodox community and other Doukhobors in an uproar. The credibility of the Crown was questioned not only by the Orthodox, who saw the trial as a "travesty," but also by the Sons of Freedom, who had risked testifying on the Crown's behalf.

The ministry agreed to my request to hire Hugh. The day after he signed on he decided to reacquaint himself with the Sons of Freedom at a Sunday *sobranya*, or prayer meeting, in Krestova, a largely Sons of Freedom community. This gathering was held in a hall, a rather rough, unfinished looking structure (at least from the outside) situated on a barren piece of land.

In the hall the men stood on one side, the women on the other. Situated between them were articles of faith – a loaf of bread, a pitcher of water, and a small jar of salt. Hugh stood with the men while psalms were sung. During one of the psalms a group of nude women entered the hall through the back door and remained out of sight until the psalm ended. The women then made their way to where Hugh was standing and abruptly announced that he and Emmett Gulley had taken their children back in the 1950s, at which point they began to remove Hugh's clothes. He resisted, explaining that he had played no part in the government's decision to apprehend their children and send them to the New Denver dormitory and explaining that he had quit his job in protest. This did nothing to dissuade the women from their mission. Hugh hoped the men standing near him would come to his aid, but not one of them moved. Finally, he let the women remove his clothes without further resistance. After he stepped out of his last remaining garment, they nudged him towards the door, with no sign of antagonism or hostility, and handed him his clothes right in front of a reporter from a local newspaper who was waiting outside. The next day Hugh made the morning headlines and I went back to my office to think about my next move. For some reason I felt exposed, and I knew I would have some explaining to do with my new boss in Victoria.

In April and May 1979 Hugh and I met with different people, looked at old files, and scanned Doukhobor reports published as far back as 1912. We attended many meetings, observed court trials, and met with various Doukhobor and knowledgeable non-Doukhobors to hear their concerns and to seek their advice.

We had heard numerous accounts of the alleged relationship between the Orthodox leadership and certain Sons of Freedom. I decided to meet with one Sons of Freedom man who had plenty of knowledge of and experience with bombings and burnings. He agreed to meet me, but only in the middle of a restaurant in the popular Yale Hotel in Grand Forks – a town that had a large Doukhobor population. Already seated, he immediately handed me a book of poems by Walt Whitman and asked me to read a certain one and tell him what it meant. This seemed rather peculiar as I knew that he had no more than a Grade 1 education, and, as I wasn't prepared to expose my ignorance so early in our relationship, I tactfully evaded the question. It took no time at all before I realized he wasn't looking for an answer but, rather, was attempting to explain to me that the instructions from the leaders to burn or bomb would be in the form of an encrypted message, no less difficult to interpret than the poem he had asked me to read. While I pondered his words he leaned towards me and said, "Let me give you one piece of advice ... you can't apply rational thinking to an irrational situation." I wasn't sure what he meant but I did recall later that, every time I or other members of the Kootenay Committee on Intergroup Relations (KCIR) would attempt to maintain order, the gathering would erupt into chaos (usually towards the end of the meeting). At first I reasoned that more structure was needed, but after a while I was no longer sure. It took a long time and I underwent many trying experiences before this man's advice triggered a sense in me that what was needed was a different, possibly creative, approach to the conflict.

Throughout these intensive five weeks it became apparent that, for over eighty years, government policy and practice towards the Doukhobors had been erratic, ranging from indifferent to punitive. Our conclusion was that the criminal justice system was neither suited to addressing the complexity of the issues nor to providing an adequate forum for responding to the questions that many Sons of Freedom and other Doukhobors were asking. We found that other forms of intervention, such as commissions of inquiry, were also ineffective with regard to resolving issues. In May 1979 I submitted our report to Mark Krasnick, recommending that the ministry appoint a local group of experienced individuals who were willing to commit their time (in this case the next eight years) to assist in unravelling this complex situation.[2]

It was 13 November 1979 when Attorney General Garde Gardom launched the Kootenay Committee on Intergroup Relations at a news conference in Cranbrook. About an hour before the announcement, the attorney general met with his district justice managers from courts, corrections, and Crown counsel, along with the subdivision commander from the Royal Canadian Mounted Police (RCMP). The district managers made it clear to him that they did not want to see a committee established because it would create more policing problems than they currently had. Although their argument was compelling, clearly they misunderstood the nature of the "problem." The attorney general then met the proposed KCIR members – Dr. Mark Mealing, a cultural anthropologist who had written about the Doukhobors; Derryl White, a historian and anthropologist who was working at Fort Steele at the time; Mel Stangeland, a psychologist from Grand Forks; Doug Feir, a former superintendent of schools; Ted Bristow, a United Church minister; Peter Abrosimoff, a court translator who had lived most of his life in Grand Forks and who knew the various factions very well; and Hugh Herbison, who had had many years of experience with the 1950 Consultative Committee on Doukhobor Affairs. It took only a few reasoned comments to convince the attorney general that this was no longer a policing problem – especially now that the Crown had failed to convict John J. Verigin – and that he needed to act right away before matters got any worse.

Although I enjoyed seeing the look on the faces of the district justice managers when the attorney general announced the formation of the KCIR, it did not make my job chairing this group any easier as they were not giving me much leeway. The reaction of the Doukhobor groups present at the Inn of the South was, to some degree, predictable: the Orthodox Doukhobors were disappointed that the KCIR was not a higher profile committee; the Reformed Doukhobors were concerned about Hugh Herbison, whom they were convinced had been responsible for the removal of their children in the mid-1950s; and the Sons of Freedom were simply looking for a forum, other than a court of law, in which they could tell their story.

Immediately following the attorney general's announcement, and for the next two years, the Reformed Doukhobors refused to participate in the KCIR, explaining that they already had a way of disseminating information about what they saw occurring. The Orthodox Doukhobors continued to push for a royal commission or, at the very least, a committee with a higher profile than the KCIR. They also wanted to be full and active members of the committee so that they could attend all the discussions and interviews.

For me, expanding the committee was not the issue. Since I presumed that it was simply a matter of time before all groups would participate within the same structure, my concern was to give the new KCIR members an opportunity to meet with individual Doukhobors in order to arrive at their own conclusions about what they perceived the issues to be. The purpose of this approach was to provide Doukhobors with an opportunity to meet with the committee without having to worry about the presence of other Doukhobors.

While the KCIR continued to meet, other events began to surface and to raise concern. In May 1980 an unexploded bomb was found on CPR rail tracks near Christina Lake. A second bomb was found near the town of Trail, and three boxes of dynamite had gone missing from a location near Rock Creek. It was never clear whether there was a link between these events, but more trouble was expected. Also during this time there were a number of Sons of Freedom women in Oakalla Prison serving a sentence for arson. The women had staged a number of hunger fasts during their incarceration, and the Sons of Freedom asked me to meet with them in order to see whether there might be a way to end their fast.

Whenever I arrived at Oakalla with Peter Abrosimoff (my translator), the director of the women's prison would take us to an old Quonset hut situated apart from the main prison population – for safety reasons (i.e., arson). Here, the women had made themselves a home. They grew vegetables in a small fenced garden just outside the hut; inside, they prepared their own special vegetarian meals in the kitchen area, which was furnished with a stove, table, and several chairs. At the other end of the hut, steel-frame beds were lined up in a row. A matron would sit at a desk just inside the entrance.

Each time we were asked to meet with the women we would enter the hut, they would greet us and then promptly remove their clothes, folding them carefully and placing them on the end of the bed. They would say a Russian prayer, and then we would get down to business. Peter and I remained dressed, while the women sat naked.[3] He would translate everything from English into Russian and vice versa. When the discussion ended, the women would dress and then serve us tea and a bowl of what they called Oakalla borscht, made from the vegetables gathered from their garden. This was the pattern that structured each of our visits.

One of the last times we visited the women at Oakalla, the usual greeting seemed strained and awkward. Then all of a sudden, out of nowhere, we heard a loud whoosh. Without any warning whatsoever, a fire had erupted around us, with bed sheets and clothes alike bursting into flames. The only entrance to the building was blocked. The matron grabbed the fire extinguisher and blasted the room. When it was over, white foam, blackened sheets, and clothes lay in a heap on the floor beneath a choking pall of acrid smoke. Through it all, the silent, "devilish" looks of the naked women remained the dominant image. Without words, the women had spoken. I decided to continue on as if nothing had happened to show them that I was serious about finding a way to end this turmoil.

Expanded Kootenay Committee on Intergroup Relations

As the Orthodox leadership continued to push for a higher profile committee, the turning point for the KCIR came in May 1981 when Robin Bourne was appointed assistant deputy minister of police services for British Columbia.[4] Robin's profile appealed to both the Reformed Doukhobors, who held anti-Soviet views, and to John Verigin and the Orthodox, which was a surprise to me, given their active involvement since the mid-1960s with Soviet officials and *Society Rodina*.[5] It was never clear to me why the Orthodox Doukhobors would be interested in someone whose past involved monitoring Soviet activities in Canada. Nevertheless, it seemed that their quest for a higher-profile committee had been successful.

Robin agreed to chair what became known as the Expanded Kootenay Committee on Intergroup Relations (EKCIR). This group's sessions involved all three Doukhobor groups (Orthodox, Reformed, and Sons of Freedom) at the same table; these groups and the former KCIR members were involved in designing the sessions. Although this was a new beginning and carried with it an element of hope, there were challenges. To begin with, in August 1982, which was about the time we were to commence the first of many EKCIR sessions, John Verigin wrote to me to express his concern regarding the two Sons of Freedom members who would be participating in the sessions. This raised the question as to "why" he was concerned, especially given that the two people about whom he was speaking were well-respected members of the Sons of Freedom. One of them had been an indicted co-conspirator during Verigin's conspiracy trial and the other was his mother, who had spent many years in prison for what she described as the "Doukhobor cause." In a letter to the author dated 25 September 1981 John Verigin again expressed concern, this time about the agenda items proposed by the Sons of Freedom. He felt that this session would "be a circus perform-ance where the criminals and culprits, fanatical zealots will have a 'hey day' with opportunity for the mass media to exploit and further en-hance the misconception that fires, arson and terrorism in general, is part of the Doukhobor doctrine." I started to sense that John J. Verigin was having second thoughts about getting to the bottom of the prob-lem that he had been pushing the government to resolve.

Mary Malakoff, a key member of the Sons of Freedom, also started to show signs of edginess. She announced two weeks prior to the sessions that she was not going to participate unless certain key individuals – namely, John Lebedoff, Anton Kolesnikoff, William Mojelski, Stephan Sorokin, and the Reformed group – all participated.[6] These were former Sons of Freedom members and, with the exception of John Lebedoff (a self-proclaimed leader of the Sons of Freedom who introduced Stephan Sorokin as the long lost Peter Verigin the Third), throughout the 1950s and 1960s had played an active leadership role in the Fraternal Council (which had been organized by Stephan Sorokin). Although I understood the importance of involving them, if the process were to work then their involvement would have to be voluntary. The objective was to have the groups co-manage the conflict rather than to put decision making in the hands of an outside authority. I hypothesized that, if this matter were to be settled, then everyone would need to commit to at-tending the EKCIR sessions. However, Mary Malakoff made it clear that more effort would be needed to ensure that this occurred.

When the first session was finally held on 28 October 1982, ironically enough, it was held at the Fireside Inn in Castlegar. There were about thirty or so people in the room sitting around an open square. At the table were members of the RCMP and the Canadian Pacific Railway Police, mayors from the local municipalities, representatives from the federal and provincial governments, six of the initial eight KCIR mem-bers,[7] and representatives from the three Doukhobor groups. Sitting outside the square were many from the Reformed and Sons of Freedom community, observing the events as they unfolded.

In planning these sessions the groups agreed that an oath should be administered, albeit on a volunteer basis, to give the meetings both structure and credibility among the Doukhobor people. A court re-corder documented each session, and transcriptions were made avail-able to the groups prior to the next session. The chair instructed each witness that, under the Canada Evidence Act, protection could not be provided should she or he give information that might prove to be self-incriminating. Finally, there was no special status given to any member, including the KCIR core members.

Everyone agreed beforehand that the subject of the initial session would be fire and security from the threat of arson. The questions to which the EKCIR sought answers included: how the use of fire began, how this use was encouraged, and what must be done to stop it. For the next four years, witness after witness described his or her experiences as a former bomber and burner.

Conclusion

Initially, the KCIR consisted of a core group of largely non-Doukhobors (with the exception of Peter Abrosimoff, who served as translator). I knew that it would be difficult to find common ground within the core group as no one, with the exception of Peter Abrosimoff, had had prior dealings with the Sons of Freedom or the Reformed Doukhobors.[8] The core group members were selected because of the skills they brought to the situation: two had training as anthropologists, one was a former superintendent of schools, one was a psychologist, and the other was a local cleric.

The first two years were frustrating for the KCIR as it continued its efforts to learn more about the nature of the Doukhobor conflict while, at the same time, trying to find ways to ward off verbal attacks from John Verigin (who was not happy with its role). While Verigin continued to pressure the attorney general to establish a commission of inquiry, the KCIR arranged meetings between Verigin and representatives of the Sons of Freedom.

The Sons of Freedom did not seem overly concerned about the membership of the KCIR. They were looking for any opportunity to tell their story and to question John Verigin as there was much confusion surrounding the recent trials and his intermediaries. The Reformed Doukhobors, on the other hand, were content not to be involved, which meant that, when issues arose, they would circulate one of their communiqués. This angered the USCC so much that it pressed the government to do something about the "hate mail" that they and others were receiving. The government did nothing as it saw this as a civil matter between the Orthodox and the Reformed Doukhobors.

By the end of the first year, Hugh Herbison was beginning to feel the pressure of the meetings and, for health reasons, decided to resign. Later, about the time the EKCIR was to meet for the first time, Doug Feir, the former superintendent of schools in Grand Forks, decided that he had had enough. This left Peter Abrosimoff and Ted Bristow, the United

Church minister, to continue on, which they did for the first two years of the EKCIR. Then they, too, decided to leave. So the two anthropologists (Derryl White and Mark Mealing) and the psychologist Mel Stangeland, along with a second psychologist (Ron Cameron) had to carry the brunt of the work. In May 1983 Peter Abrosimoff was replaced by Jack McIntosh, an archivist from UBC who had lived in the Kootenays, was familiar with the Doukhobor material in Special Collections at UBC's Main Library, and could speak and write Russian.

The challenge for me during these first two years was to keep the attorney general focused on continuing with the KCIR. The other challenge was to keep the Reformed Doukhobors informed in the hope that they might agree to join the other groups while, at the same time, not being perceived as supporting one group over another.

The turning point for the Reformed Doukhobors and the USCC occurred when Robin Bourne was introduced to them. Robin, as the new assistant deputy minister for Police Services, provided an element of leadership credibility, which, until then, had been missing. I worked with Robin and the groups over the next several months to create a structure acceptable both to the groups and to the ministry.

Notwithstanding all the pressure, the upside for the first two years was that the KCIR used its time to interview people on their own (i.e., without the groups being present). It also used this time to gain access to archival materials as it searched for evidence that would provide new insights into the stories its members had been hearing. By the time the EKCIR sessions began, the core group had amassed a fair collection of archival materials from UBC as well as from the provincial archives in Victoria, RCMP headquarters, and the federal archives in Ottawa, all of which proved to be of benefit when the committee made its presentation.

4
Competing Narratives

For decades, the Orthodox Doukhobors had been demanding that the provincial government end the terrorism by ridding their community of the Sons of Freedom. The Sons of Freedom argued that the Orthodox leadership encouraged them to burn and bomb. This was part of the narrative exchange that had taken place off and on over several decades and that was brought to a head during the Expanded Kootenay Committee on Intergroup Relations (EKCIR) sessions. These sessions officially began on 28 October 1982 and were documented by a court recorder who attended all of them.

The sessions themselves were held approximately three to four times a year. During each session the Doukhobor groups presented witnesses who told of their experiences of being either victims or perpetrators of burning and bombing. Between each session a smaller planning group, made up of EKCIR core members and representatives from the Doukhobor groups, met to discuss the key issues that had arisen and to plan for the next session.

In reading through the EKCIR transcripts I realized that what was missing was the pitch and accent of the voices, the amusing moments and self-deprecating humour displayed in jokes told by community members during the breaks. Also missing were the deep, rich, resonating a cappella tones that surged through every one of us the moment the Doukhobor people began to sing. Initially, singing was not a part of the EKCIR sessions, but somewhere near the mid-point of the process, when discussions had reached a certain pitch and intensity, one of the Doukhobor delegates suggested that a traditional hymn be sung by those present. This had an amazing effect with regard to altering the tone of the discussions. Subsequently, this technique was to be used to create a sense of harmony on various occasions when discussions went awry.

Prior to the first session (28 and 29 October 1982), the Union of Spiritual Communities of Christ (USCC) circulated among the participants a written brief entitled *The Thorny Pathway,* which had been prepared for a meeting between the Orthodox Doukhobors and the attorney general. The brief described how the Sons of Freedom had victimized the Orthodox Doukhobors, and how the Orthodox leader, John J. Verigin, was then later victimized by the justice system. It described Mr. Verigin's trial as a "totally unwarranted humiliation" that was based "on false charges of conspiracy brought on by self-confessed terrorists and arsonists who are still free and at large."[1] It further stated that all of the property that had been destroyed had fallen victim to the same terrorist faction. And it concluded that

> all of these actions point to the inept way in which the terrorist problem has been handled in the Kootenay and Boundary areas by the authorities directly concerned with the situation. Their method of approach to this problem also shows lack of understanding of the facts relating to the terrorist activities in these areas and also their lack of knowledge about the peaceful and productive history of the Union of Spiritual Communities of Christ membership and its leadership.

The brief also described the numerous efforts the Orthodox Doukhobors had made to convince the provincial government of the need to establish a royal commission in order to solve the Doukhobor problem. The underlying concern of the Orthodox Doukhobors was to find some form of relief from the escalating insurance costs and from the twenty-four-hour watch they had been maintaining on all of their community holdings, including John Verigin's home. The brief represented what the USCC believed were the "facts," which, as it indicated, were for others to disprove.

The first session of the EKCIR began with John Verigin's asking, on behalf of the USCC, for everyone to trust them. He said that the USCC "record would show that we are deserving of your trust," which, he added, "is a matter of life and death."[2] Mr. Verigin's comments were at times conciliatory, noting that those who had committed unacceptable acts had suffered through their incarceration. He said that, although fire was used to destroy firearms at an event known as the "burning of the arms" in Russia in 1895, the use of fire in Canada had never been part of Doukhobor philosophy or practice. His conciliatory tone soon changed when he referred to the use of fire as an "act of either a mentally deranged person or a religious fanatic who seeks the achievement of his own or their own aims."[3]

Following Mr. Verigin, Fred Makortoff, representing the Reformed Doukhobors,[4] suggested that bombings and arson were not solely the responsibility of the Sons of Freedom but, rather, involved what he referred to as "community" members. In other words, he believed that Orthodox members had played a part in these events. Mr. Makortoff said that he planned to approach the sessions by having the Sons of Freedom describe their involvement in the burnings and bombings and then having them give their reasons for such actions.

Fred Makortoff asserted that "a Doukhobor's life is an act of faith in the leadership" and that their dependence on their leaders "virtually precluded their thinking in definite terms about their future."[5] This meant that the Doukhobors didn't question who or what they were because everyone believed that "the leaders knew what they were doing as they held divine wisdom in these matters."[6] He described the Reformed Doukhobors as those who had participated in bombings and burnings and who "were a constant source of embarrassment to fellow Canadians." "Ideas of this nature," he added, were "embedded so deeply and held so fiercely," and he noted that nothing of what they did was done for personal gain.[7]

Unlike John Verigin's opening comments, which appeared directed towards the non-Doukhobor members at the table, Fred Makortoff's comments seemed to speak to Doukhobor people in general, asking them to judge for themselves the information presented:

> Let us all strive to maintain objectivity and a sense of purpose. Only then with our shared views as brushes and colours, adding one to the other, can we hope to paint a picture of the reality of the situation we all wish to understand. This painting may not necessarily agree with any one view and if viewed through coloured glasses to some may appear stark or harsh. We are not here to crucify anyone nor to manufacture heroes. If, in our commonly held view, any group or individual appears in the relative terms of good or bad, then so be it.[8]

Makortoff knew that reaching the general public would be the biggest challenge as most Doukhobor and local non-Doukhobor people had already made up their minds. He believed that what was needed was to convince both the Reformed and the Sons of Freedom that the time had come to put responsibility where it belonged: at the feet of the Orthodox leadership. If he could convince the Sons of Freedom to come forward, as he and Stephan Sorokin had done prior to the John Verigin trial, then maybe his and others' efforts could create the conditions for change.

Mr. Makortoff described the EKCIR forum as "the round table" that everyone had been waiting for, which was his way of acknowledging certain stories and prophesies that had been told in the past about a gathering that would be held to account for all the suffering that people had endured. In describing this event he struck a note of caution when he suggested that Doukhobor people had witnessed similar events, such as the Blakemore, Sullivan, and Lord commissions of inquiry, in which outsiders had sat in judgment. In all cases this had worsened rather than resolved the problem.

In concluding his opening remarks the chair, Robin Bourne, described his role as facilitative rather than authoritative, and he indicated that, from time to time, he would ask for everyone's advice regarding whether he was "being too arbitrary or too lenient or fair or unfair."[9] Overall, the chair managed to set a tone that remained consistent throughout the next five years.

Subjugate Narratives
The first witness presented by the Reformed Doukhobors was Nick Nevokshonoff,[10] who spoke in Russian about a rash of fires that destroyed a number of schools one evening in 1924.[11] He said that there were times when "not only the Sons of Freedom ... were involved in the act of fire ... [but there were] different times when people from other groups, community people, members of the Christian Community of Universal Brotherhood (CCUB Ltd.) and also the independent farmers took part [as well]."[12]

[In] 1924, in one night, schools burned [in] all the settlements of the members of the Christian Community of Universal Brotherhood. Seven schools in this district and the burning of these schools, they were dispatched with by the members of the Community people themselves without any Sons of Freedom taking part. This happened at Easter when the teachers were all away at home. In every district there were members elected for one year as trustees in regards to the community affairs. They were called elders. There was one elder that was elected that was the head of all the other elders. The one that was serving without being changed ... From time to time he went throughout the villages ... overseeing the activities of different villages. Coming through the villages

just before Easter ... [he] told every elder of the village, at a certain time
of the night at Easter that a school must be burned.[13]

Nick Nevokshonoff said that he remembered the names of all the elders
and their helpers. He believed that the fires were the result of people
retaliating for the way they were being treated by the government. He
suggested that all Doukhobors perceived schools as militaristic, with
flag raising, queuing, marching, and similar activities being practised –
to which their faith was opposed. To illustrate the point, Mr. Makortoff
read from a Doukhobor psalm sung by all Doukhobor groups:

> Question: Why do you not attend English schools and learn grammar?
> Answer: Schools prepare children for killing and wars. All your edu-
> cated children do not live with their parents and do not respect them.
> We are striving to learn in the school of God's nature, which gives us
> knowledge of the godly beauty of the universe, in order to love the
> world, which is created by God for our joy. At the same time, we, to-
> gether with our parents, are striving to gain sustenance for our flesh
> from the soil with our own labours ... I think the fact that the majority
> of elder Doukhobors are illiterate speaks for itself.[14]

This, he suggested, meant that all Doukhobors share similar beliefs.

Makortoff also read from a newspaper clipping from 17 May 1923,
which referred to some Doukhobor families' having been fined $300 for
not sending their children to school. And he read from a letter that was
sent by Samuel Verishagin, who was responsible for all matters pertaining to education in the CCUB Ltd., to the provincial government, stating: "We cannot guarantee that the schools will not be burned."[15] Many
believed that Peter V. Verigin had instructed Mr. Verishagin to write this
letter.

John Verigin accepted that it was Peter V. Verigin's instructions that
led to the writing of the letter. He also accepted that the letter infers
that Peter V. Verigin "cannot guarantee that schools will not be burned";
however, he insisted that the letter nowhere suggests that "Peter V.
Verigin was launching a campaign of burning schools."[16] In response,
Mr. Makortoff stated that "by Peter Verigin's own words, there [were]
perhaps twenty, maybe thirty Sons of Freedom then. Means of getting
about were difficult; the roads weren't what they are now,"[17] and the
Sons of Freedom did not have access to transportation. His conclusion
was that the elder appointed by Peter V. Verigin would know who was
involved in burning schools because he was the only one with access to

transportation and, thus, the only one who could travel between the communities. Although there were gaps in the evidence, it did raise new questions.

At the end of the first day, John Verigin appeared impatient and suggested that it was historians who should be listening to these stories: "If we are going to look into the history ... I think we're going to ... be here for too long and no one of us wishes to do that."[18] He suggested that "as true Christians, or possibly as true Doukhobors, let all of us together give ourselves a commitment [that] no matter who was responsible in the past for these fires ... we recognize that it is wrong and we don't want ... to commit arson any further."[19] He proposed that if everyone signed a declaration there would be no further need for arson and the matter would be settled. The chair, however, was not convinced that signing a declaration would end the turmoil, and he suggested that there was still more to learn.

Mr. Makortoff reminded Mr. Verigin that, for many decades, the Doukhobor people had been "talking about a promised time and a 'round table.'"[20] This, he added, was the time "when all their loyalties and trust in their leadership and all their suffering would be accounted for."[21]

Many believed that the Verigin leadership held the key to the "truth." They assumed that, since he had demanded such a forum, the time had come for the truth to be told, which, for the Sons of Freedom, meant that their role in saving "Doukhoborism" would be recognized (if not understood) once and for all.

The next Sons of Freedom witness was William Stupnikoff,[22] who talked about living in Saskatchewan in the 1930s, when four men from British Columbia came to him and others to explain why there was a need to destroy schools. One of the men was Peter N. Maloff,[23] who was considered a close associate of Peter Petrovich Verigin (Peter V. Verigin's son), whom they referred to as *Chistiakov.*[24] Mr. Stupnikoff explained the link between Chistiakov and the Sons of Freedom, referring to God's law as "green lights" and government's law as "red lights." He said he had been taught to believe that the red lights were forced upon them, and he used Mr. Nevokshonoff's reference to the burning of schools as an example. "Red lights" meant that they had to "remove it from its place."[25] "Removing the trouble" meant destroying a building or some other structure that presented a "problem" to the Doukhobor people.

Cryptic and Symbolic Language

Throughout most of the ECKIR sessions the cryptic and symbolic language used to convey messages was a topic of discussion. For example,

on day two of the first session the discussion drifted from the presentations to Alex Gritchin, one of the USCC executive members, who had
worn a red shirt to a recent gathering to which some Sons of Freedom
members had been invited. Olga Hoodicoff, a Sons of Freedom member, said that Alex Gritchin knows that red, whether worn as a shirt, tie,
or whatever, would be taken by the Sons of Freedom as a signal to burn.
She asked Mr. Gritchin why he wore a red shirt that evening. He explained that it was simply a gift and nothing more, which led to an
exchange between Mr. Gritchin and Mark Mealing, a KCIR member.
Although there was no way to determine what Mr. Gritchin's intention
was at the time, the incident left Mark Mealing questioning why, given
what he knew about the Sons of Freedom, he would wear what he did.

> Dr. Mealing: We've heard continually ... heartfelt complaints of USCC
> members and executive members that the Sons of Freedom are wrong,
> they include criminals, they include psychotics, they are a very small
> part of the Doukhobor population, less than one percent. They are
> on the wrong path, they are not to be trusted, as you said.
> Mr. Gritchin: I didn't say not to be trusted.
> Dr. Mealing: No, what you said was that anything may be twisted and
> taken as a signal. And I'm really concerned that nevertheless, mem-
> bers of the USCC, in their executive positions, knowing that any-
> thing may be misinterpreted, put themselves in a position privately
> as well as publicly where such interpretations may be made. If you
> know that the Sons of Freedom have a certain feeling about a red pen
> or a red shirt, why in heaven's sake wear it when you go to meet
> them? And why go to meet them wearing that?
> Mr. Gritchin: It was given to me as a present and there's nothing wrong
> with that, to wear a red shirt. And I was never told not to wear one.
> Dr. Mealing: You were not told not to wear one, Mr. Gritchin, but you
> know yourself and you've just said that such things may be interpreted.
> Mr. Gritchin: After this incident, yes, when she told me. Now, damn
> right, I'll never wear it in front of her.[26]

Olga Hoodicoff continued her questioning of the USCC, this time asking why it sent a letter to the Sons of Freedom in August 1972[27] (while
they were camped outside of Agassiz Mountain Prison), with a red peace
dove on the letterhead, which she said was usually blue. Mr. Verigin
explained that it was a mistake made by the company from which they
ordered the letterhead rather than an intended act on the part of the
USCC.

When the committee asked Ms. Hoodicoff whether she thought Mr. Verigin had the ability to place a curse on her, she replied that he did. In response to whether he had the power to place a curse on her now, she replied that he did. "Was she concerned about giving her story to the KCIR, knowing that he still had the power?" she was asked. "Yes," she answered, but she wanted her involvement in the burnings to come to an end so that "her children don't have to go through what [she] had been going through and what [her] mother has been going through [all these years]."[28]

Another example of the use of cryptic and symbolic language was provided by Polly Chernoff, who had spent many years in prison for setting fires and who told the ECKIR that she and other Sons of Freedom women "sacrificed not only their material possessions but the best part of their lives to keep the name Doukhobor alive."[29] She said that she received messages from Peter Legebokoff, a former editor of *Iskra* (a USCC publication), in the form of parables that were included in the body of his publication. These were parables that others would not understand as they were intended for specific individuals, mostly Sons of Freedom members. She also received other messages, some of which were typewritten, while others were written by hand. The handwritten messages were usually signed P.L., which she believed stood for Peter Legebokoff. To give credence to her story Fred Makortoff read out one of the messages she had received: "It is time to begin work, enough sleep. It is time to rise and start singing a hymn. It is time to rise brothers, the hour has come to repair the home of David. Walk out onto an open road saying that you, your children will be meeting you in tears. Do not be thieves. Just thank the star. It is time. It is time. May God help you."[30]

Mr. Verigin asked why Ms. Chernoff assumed that the messages were from the Orthodox Doukhobors as a whole. She said that Mr. Legebokoff, who played a prominent role as editor of *Iskra*, would be representing the larger community. But she admitted that she did not have any evidence to back up her story. Mr. Verigin then asked, "are you trying to suggest to me that without any rhyme or reason, Peter Legebokoff singled you out, Polly Chernoff, [and] could [you] possibly explain what relationship or what association with Peter Legebokoff did you have outside of these letters?" "I never spoke to him and I never spoke to you," she replied.[31]

Further confusion over the intent of messages was highlighted when Sam Konkin described John Verigin's visit to the Sons of Freedom in Agassiz on 7 March 1973. He said that Mr. Verigin told the "Freedomites" that "we have land for you ... but you must be ready for the land and the land will be ready for you."[32] Mr. Konkin said that the Sons of Freedom well understood what Mr. Verigin had in mind. He was telling them to start making trouble, which he said meant bombing and burning. At the time many of the Sons of Freedom did not want further trouble because they had spent time in prison, some had lost their families, and others had lost their health. "Besides," Mr. Konkin added, "they had very little to burn in Agassiz as they were living in tarpaper shacks."[33] When Mr. Verigin left, the Sons of Freedom decided to send a delegation to his home to tell him that they did not want any further trouble but that they did need land for people to live upon. However, Mr. Konkin added, he refused to meet with them. According to Mr. Konkin, it was soon after the delegation returned to Agassiz that Mr. Verigin sent them the letter with the red peace dove. Mr. Konkin concluded that, to the "Sons of Freedom, red dove was the signal from Verigin to start trouble."[34]

Doukhobor Lands
Doukhobor land was an ongoing issue for the Sons of Freedom, especially for those who were living in "tar-paper shacks" outside of Agassiz Mountain Prison. In a letter they sent to John Verigin on 2 November 1971 they expressed concern not only that Mr. Verigin had not welcomed the delegation that went to meet with him but also that their toil and suffering were not being recognized, especially when it came to land. "We believed you that land should not be bought or sold, when the Canadian government intended to sell it to us, and if not to us then to non-Doukhobors."[35] The letter goes on to state:

> We fulfilled everything, burned homes on these lands in order to stop the selling and buying of community lands. Not only once, you have stated that if we buy community land into private property, it is finished for the community and Doukhoborism. Now we hear that John J. bought more land than anyone else, alone.[36]

By the mid-1970s resentment of John Verigin was mounting and, over the next few years, the Sons of Freedom gave statements to the RCMP regarding his role behind the scenes.

Retaliation for Peter the Lordly's Death
At the December 1982 EKCIR session Sam Konkin explained that the Sons of Freedom believed that the government had killed Peter V. Verigin in 1924 by means of a Canadian Pacific Railway train explosion. He and

other Sons of Freedom were told that, if they sent their children to school or purchased former Doukhobor lands,[37] then they would have the "blood of Lordly Verigin" over them. "Bombing and burning were a means of purifying and making you worthy," he said. When asked what he meant by this he said he was told that "if you believe in your leader and you do what he tells you ... he will save you."[38] He suggested that following orders was considered an act of selflessness that would lead to some form of future redemption.

At the session held in February 1983 William Hremakin[39] read a statement about his involvement in bombings since the 1940s. Mr. Hremakin was the person the Sons of Freedom would go to for dynamite. He was twenty years old when he was "appointed," and he said he was unable to refuse. Mr. Hremakin (who was ninety-four years old in 1982), like Mr. Konkin, explained that bombings were the result of the government's having killed Peter the Lordly Verigin in the 1924 CPR train explosion.

Mr. Hremakin said he was told that the Doukhobors were to "erect a pillar of fire from the ground up to heaven."[40] Although he did not explain what this meant, he assumed that it was his role to comply with whatever instructions he received. As an example, he described the burning of the Doukhobor jam factory in Brilliant on 12 December 1943. He said he received instructions to torch this building from John Zbitnoff,[41] who told him that these instructions were being passed to him from the "highest" (in this case, John Verigin). When he asked why it was necessary to destroy this building, he said John Zbitnoff told him that the "government wants to make this factory a soldier's hospital or a war-warehouse."[42]

There were other occasions throughout the EKCIR sessions when both cryptic messages and Peter the Lordly's death were used to justify some particular action. For example, at the December 1982 session Mary Astoforoff, a Sons of Freedom member who had spent many years in and out of jail, mentioned the Doukhobor Museum across from the airport in Castlegar: "Out of the holy community which was under the leadership of the holy prophet and Saviour Peter the Lordly, they created an icon, museum, but his truth, love, trample under their feet ... he who is building the museum, he is bringing suffering on the Doukhobors ... For it is said, this museum is condemned to fire."[43] The museum was set ablaze a short time later and Mary Astoforoff was one of two Sons of Freedom women arrested at the scene, where she and others were standing naked waiting for the police and fire trucks to arrive. Why the museum was a target, especially after all these years, no one would say.

What happened over those past few months that led the women to think that the museum was now an "icon" that needed to be destroyed? The Sons of Freedom were looking for answers from Harry Voykin,[44] who operated a restaurant next to the museum. Many of the Sons of Freedom who had been invited to his restaurant thought he might have something to do with this particular fire. The two women arrested did not say anything other than that the water had been turned off before they arrived, which they claim resulted in a much larger fire than they had intended. This led to more confusion and more unanswered questions.

Although the EKCIR learned that many of the bombings were in retaliation for Peter the Lordly's death and that a number of burnings were in reaction to the policies of the provincial government (e.g., enforced schooling), some remained unexplained. For instance, at one session John Savinkoff, a Sons of Freedom member from Gilpin, read a statement concerning those he knew to be responsible for destroying the Grand Forks Co-op and post office, Stephan Sorokin's trailer home, and the Grand Forks and Brilliant cultural centres during the mid-1970s. He admitted to being the one who organized the women to burn Sorokin's home, which, he claims, was done for the salvation of all Doukhobors. However, he alleged that it was at John Verigin's instructions that these fires were lit and that if he had not carried this out he would have been "cursed" for seven generations.

Mr. Savinkoff never said where or when he received his instructions from John Verigin. He did say, however, that his son and Peter Astoforoff met with John Verigin at a restaurant in Grand Forks where the latter described himself as the "head" and Peter Astoforoff[45] as the "manager." Peter Savinkoff, John Savinkoff's son, was described as the "worker." Mr. Savinkoff said that his son was told by John Verigin that, whatever Peter Astoforoff told him or others to do, they were to do it, which they did, thus implying that they had destroyed the Grand Forks Co-op, the former post office, and the Grand Forks Cultural Centre.[46]

Many of the Sons of Freedom said they participated in bombings and arson not because of Peter the Lordly's death or government policy but because of their fear of being "cursed" by the Orthodox leadership. John Verigin described this as an excuse conjured up by the Sons of Freedom and that the "curse" had no place in Doukhobor culture. He said that the notion of the curse was introduced simply to confuse the weary listener. This story was also presented at Mr. Verigin's trial, where, under cross-examination, it was discounted for lack of corroborating evidence.

Intimidation

Not all of the burnings were the result of someone having received instructions; sometimes the setting of a fire was an individual's way of saving Doukhoborism. Polly Chernoff, a Sons of Freedom member, talked about all of the suffering that goes on in this world and spoke of her strong desire to help end it. The Sons of Freedom saw themselves as helping to relieve suffering through sacrifice. In 1962, while she was in prison, the prison doctor told her that hunger fasts (which were common among Sons of Freedom inmates) were ruining her health.[47] This was when she decided she had had enough of fires and prison. Then, in 1975, fire ravaged her garage and she almost lost her children.

> Somebody tried to set it up ... as though I [was responsible]. That night, thank goodness that my husband was so mad at me that he wouldn't go to bed. He just sat there reading papers. And so I went to bed ... And when he came to bed, our daughter-in-law came screaming that there was a fire. Well ... it wasn't only the garage, it was a workshop that they built, a new workshop and there were a couple of rooms there for my husband's mother and her son to live with us. And our son and our son-in-law had windows and doors and everything for a house in there; and it was ... packed full. [The room] was so small that anything that was good, you know, we had in there. Everything went up in flames. Then we came out. The garage that we were living in, it was catching fire. And thank goodness she [daughter-in-law] knew what to do. She says, "You take ... all those clothes off the line and dip them in water and hand them to me." As soon as the wall starts smoking, she'd put ... these blankets over and by that time the rest of the blankets would be smoking. So, she'd dip those and that's how she saved [the building]. And two of the children were right under ... that wall. If it weren't for her, we'd all have been gone.[48]

Ms. Chernoff said that for about a year her daughter-in-law slept in her jeans because she was afraid that it might happen again. Ms. Chernoff knew that the fire was a warning to her to continue her involvement. "So, when this happened, I says, I'll go back to jail, I don't care, even if I'm not well. I'll rot in jail so they wouldn't touch my children."[49] So she went and burned again.

Soon after Ms. Chernoff returned from jail she was pressured to continue the burnings, but she decided that she did not want to do this. Her son had just finished building his house, which was located nearby, when one of the rooms where the children were sleeping was set ablaze.

She could hear the dog barking outside her door, and when she opened the door to let him in "he just flew down to their house and showed me just where this fire was."[50] This time it was right under the kids' bedroom.

> I tried to wake them up and I couldn't ... And so when my husband saw that I didn't come back, he came out and of course, you know, they put out the fire. The jar melted and there were footsteps there and the police came and they didn't do nothing about it ... To this day, ... every night several times a night, we get up and walk around the house.[51]

When Ms. Chernoff told her story there was an eerie atmosphere in the room, as though her story was not so much for us as it was for her husband John, who sat off to her side. Was this her way of atoning for all the years she had dedicated herself to "the cause"? And would her story enable her to finally end her involvement in burnings? The short answer is that, since 1980, she has not participated in any further burnings acts, nor have there been any further acts of arson directed towards her or her son's homes.

Intimidation between Sessions

There were times when intimidation of witnesses was reported to have occurred between EKCIR sessions. For instance, on 31 May 1983 Robin Bourne reported on two matters that had been brought to his attention. The first occurred when two individuals approached the wife of one of the witnesses, Sam Konkin,[52] and made the following comment: "Sam had a good business and a good life and perhaps he shouldn't talk so much."[53] Also, someone telephoned Mr. Konkin to tell him that the May EKCIR session had been cancelled (which was not true).

The second matter involved John Verigin and his allegation that Mr. Elasoff, whom he presumed was the same Mr. Elasoff[54] who was a member of the Reformed Sons of Freedom, had been in Grand Forks and was heard to say, "I'm going to kill Verigin." The chair of the committee reported that, soon after the matter was raised, Mr. Elasoff swore an affidavit indicating that he had never made such a remark. Mr. Verigin confirmed that it was a different Mr. Elasoff who had made the remark and apologized for the problem he had caused.

On another occasion, in giving testimony John Savinkoff, a witness for the Reformed Sons of Freedom, asked the chair if he could question Peter Astoforoff, who was reading a prepared statement for Mr. Savinkoff. The chair agreed.[55] Mr. Savinkoff asked Peter Astoforoff if John Verigin had asked to meet with him before the session. Mr. Astoforoff said that he had. "And, [when you met with him], what did he ask you to do?" Mr. Savinkoff inquired.[56] "He asked me so I would say that I had falsely accused him, and so I would say before the people that he had not instructed me."[57] "Is it the truth that he did not instruct you or is it the truth that he did instruct you?" asked Mr. Savinkoff. "He was asking me so I would say he did not instruct me," he replied.[58] Nothing more was said either by Mr. Astoforoff or by Mr. Verigin.

Refurbishing the Historical Record

After three sessions and after having heard witnesses from the Reformed and Sons of Freedom groups, it was time for John Verigin and the USCC to make their presentation. John Verigin began by reminding everyone that "the USCC delegation represents the greatest number of people in relationship to the other groups present"[59] and that the USCC had suffered from years of terrorism. He suggested that the Sons of Freedom had a "May day in presenting and repeating evidences, testimony of hearsay innuendoes, allegations and everything."[60] He indicated that the media added "insult to injury" for his members when they reported that the "leaders should share the blame for these fires being perpetuated from the start."[61]

> Never had Peter Lordly, never had Peter Chistiakov, never had I, in the sense of leaders of the Doukhobors, gave [sic] any instructions to burn or to bomb. And we'd like this to be clearly understood that the previous record and testimony that was given, it was the testimony, as I said, of allegation, second-hand, third-hand; sometimes and we still are waiting if the onus is that a person is innocent until proven guilty, we are still waiting for evidence to show to that effect ... please don't swallow hook, line, and sinker the information that was presented because it still has to be verified, corroborated.[62]

Again, Mr. Verigin seemed more interested in addressing the non-Doukhobor people who were present than in addressing the Doukhobors. He seemed particularly interested in addressing the mayors representing the four surrounding municipalities. He read from *The Thorny Pathway*, the report that he had presented on the first day of the proceedings in October 1982, highlighting the overall concerns of the USCC regarding the years of terrorism. He described the USCC's need to be protected from terrorists and from the hate literature that had been circulating. He mentioned some concerns his organization was having with regard to education, "land claims," government grants, pensions, social welfare, and the need to be secure from destruction and intimidation (the result of which was being exacerbated by mounting insurance costs). He concluded that the USCC had lost confidence in the RCMP and that, therefore, a royal commission was needed to end the terrorism.

Following his presentation Mr. Verigin called Lucy Maloff, the wife of Peter N. Maloff, a respected Doukhobor philosopher, as a witness to tell her side of the story concerning statements made at earlier sessions by Sons of Freedom witnesses. In her statement (read by her son) she told the committee that her husband had been portrayed as Peter Chistiakov Verigin's "faithful stooge, his right-hand man, in carrying Verigin's message to the Freedomites,"[63] which she claimed was not true. She said she recalled the words of Peter P. Verigin, who in many of his speeches and public appearances chastised the fanatical acts of the Sons of Freedom: "He warned the Doukhobors to steer clear of such elements and provocateurs, hiding as wolves in sheep's clothing amongst the Sons of Freedom."[64] Ms. Maloff described her husband as an idealist, a life-time vegetarian who corresponded with Mahatma Gandhi in India; John Haynes Holmes, a Community Church minister in New York; A.J. Muste, a world-renowned pacifist and idealist; and Rabindranath Tagore, one of India's great poets and a Nobel laureate. She denied that her deceased husband had participated with the Sons of Freedom in nude parades or arson.

Following her statement, Ms. Maloff was asked by Fred Makortoff if her husband had ever spent time in jail. She said that she and her husband had been sent to Piers Island, across from Victoria, in 1932 for opposing the war. Mary Malakoff, a Sons of Freedom representative, pointed out that all of those sentenced to Piers Island were convicted of nudity rather than of opposing the war (which makes sense, given that no war was being conducted at that time and that none was foreseen). Ms. Maloff explained that both she and her husband were innocent, as were the others who were sentenced to Piers Island. Her comment created an uneasy stir among the Sons of Freedom present in the room.

When asked whether her husband had any connections to the Sons of Freedom, she replied that he had no association with them as they lived some distance away. Derryl White, one of the core KCIR members, read to her a passage from a 1950 paper written by Peter N. Maloff entitled "A Report on the Doukhobors," which had been prepared for Harry Hawthorn's research committee, and he asked her to clarify what her husband might have meant. In his report Peter Maloff said that the surprising thing about the Orthodox Doukhobors was that they were "pointing an accusing finger at the Sons of Freedom for the same work they themselves started and maintained for many years."

> This moral cowardice of the former community members is nothing less than betrayal of the Doukhobor cause. Their life is full of contradiction and this continuous shifting from left to right and vice versa, whenever it suits their purpose, this shifting back and forth in regards to Doukhobor ideology has a profound influence on the Sons of Freedom movement, because of such shifting, they either give a substantial support to Sons of Freedom or prompt them to the extremes.[65]

After parts of the report were read to her, Lucy Maloff said that she did not think her husband would write such a thing. Jack McIntosh, who was an archivist at the University of British Columbia and worked in the Doukhobor special collections section, drew to her attention that the paper was part of a collection of her husband's writings. The question was, how was it that she was not informed about her husband's writings or about his knowledge of and relationship with the Sons of Freedom? For example, in his *In Quest of a Solution (Three Reports on Doukhobor Problem)*, which he wrote in 1957, he talked about his years of experience with both the Orthodox and Sons of Freedom Doukhobors. Here, he states that the "Doukhobors themselves did much to create the problem,"[66] arguing that therefore they could not regard themselves as innocent of the violence that had been occurring. He eventually isolates himself from all the groups, noting in his second report, *An Open Letter Addressed to All Concerned with the Doukhobor Problem*, "my voluntary alienation was because the Doukhobors in general are not telling the whole truth."[67]

After listening to Lucy Maloff's exchange with members of the EKCIR, what became evident to me was that her statement had been written by someone else and that her responses to questions were intended to craft a certain impression – one that differed from those made by people who knew Peter Maloff or other members of her family. For example, when asked if her son had been in jail for nudity in 1944, she claimed that he had not, at which point Mr. Makortoff produced a news article describing her son's arrest. It was not clear whether her refusal to acknowledge her husband's relationship with the Sons of Freedom was her idea or someone else's.

Creating Dissonance to Effect Change

In the June 1983 EKCIR session Fred Makortoff commented that he had observed positive changes occurring at recent sessions, noting that these were subtle but important as they were changing the perceptions that some members had of the other groups. However, these changes in perception did not last long. At the beginning of the next session, which was held in July 1983, whatever changes that had occurred were no longer evident. The Sons of Freedom were focusing on the Reformed Doukhobors, rather than on the Orthodox leadership, as the reason for the havoc among Sons of Freedom members.

Fred Makortoff tried to divert the discussion back to the USCC by openly questioning the Sons of Freedom strategy. He reminded the Sons of Freedom that Peter Astoforoff had admitted that, prior to an earlier session, he had been asked by John Verigin to change his story. Mr. Makortoff asked Peter Astoforoff why he was no longer pursuing the USCC leadership. "We've had a witness presented here by the Sons of Freedom, one Harry Voykin, whose testimony was very contradictory. And we're wondering if, for instance, Harry Voykin's testimony, if that had been pursued, it would throw a great deal of light as to why Mr. Astoforoff's mother[68] at this point in time is throwing up with blood and is on her death bed."[69] Clearly, his comments were intended to provoke the Sons of Freedom, especially Peter Astoforoff, to speak out. The response Mr. Makortoff had hoped for, however, was not forthcoming – at least not at the time.

Later that day there was an exchange between Sam Konkin and Peter Astoforoff concerning a story that Mr. Konkin had told about meeting Peter Astoforoff in Kamloops. After listening for awhile, Mr. Astoforoff said that Mr. Konkin had made up parts of the story and he wanted to know who had put him up to it. The chair asked Mr. Astoforoff if he was "playing some sort of game with Mr. Konkin." Mr. Astoforoff, now riled, explained that he was offended by Mr. Makortoff's earlier comments, which had insinuated that the Sons of Freedom "are the cause of mother being in jail and suffering now and spitting blood, because we will not bring Harry Voykin and question him."[70] Mel Stangeland, a core KCIR member, saw this as an opportunity to ask Mr. Astoforoff about Mr. Verigin's previous insistence that he had never instructed him to burn.

> The only time that I received instructions from Verigin was ... when the USCC Hall was burnt and when there was an attempted arson on the post office. I passed on those messages to the boys that I had received them from Verigin, but no other messages. I was never involved with dynamite.[71]

Bourne asked whether or not these were the instructions he had actually received, and Mr. Astoforoff replied, "From Mr. Verigin, yeah ..."[72] This led to an exchange between Peter Astoforoff and John Verigin regarding the former's allegation that Mr. Verigin had instructed him to destroy various buildings. During this exchange Mr. Verigin attempted to "cross-examine" Mr. Astoforoff.

> Mr. Verigin: When and in whose presence ... were these instructions given?
>
> Mr. Astoforoff: These instructions I heard from you was after you and I spent several hours in the beer parlor at the Grand Forks Hotel. I suppose we could get about fifty witnesses that were there to attest to the fact that you and I sat there drinking beer. After a few beers, you got into my truck and you asked me to take you home or I asked you if you had a ride and you said, no. I don't know which exactly. We got into my truck, my pick-up, which was red by the way and you got into it. And away we went. I was taking you home ... Just across the cemetery, as we were driving up, the USCC cemetery, you said, "Well, now you have to listen, this and this and this." In fact, you name three buildings. It was either your house, your personal dwelling, the USCC –
>
> Mr. Verigin: ... Would you please recollect exactly the words or expression that I used to you? Exactly what words?
>
> Mr. Astoforoff: It happened a few years ago. I have it in my statement, if you want the exact words, I'd have to read the statement.
>
> Mr. Verigin: This statement, you introduced into evidence at the trial against me?
>
> Mr. Astoforoff: That's right. Those were the exact words, but I'm saying I got from you instructions to burn down one of the three buildings. Later, I had – I had instructions from you, you say, the cultural center and I say, "There isn't one in town that I know of." And ... you say, "Yes there is." So, I didn't know what building you meant until I relayed the message to Mr. Savinkoff. I guess at his place. And he says, "Take a look at the [news]paper ... The post office is slated to be a cultural center and that must be the building he meant."

Here, Mr. Verigin, in his effort to clarify the situation, gave the EKCIR reason to believe that he had met with Mr. Astoforoff on at least two different occasions.

Mr. Verigin: Mr. Chairman, he's referring to two different circumstances, as I understand. One was by the cemetery –

Mr. Astoforoff: In my pick-up.

Mr. Verigin: – on my pick-up. Now, where was this other incident about the cultural center, which is supposedly the post office?

Mr. Astoforoff: John Pankoff's service station that's the one that was right across from the Grand Forks Hotel.

Mr. Verigin: John Pankoff's service station?

Mr. Astoforoff: I think it was.

Mr. Verigin: May I correct you? Your memory seems to be very hazy. You see, John Pankoff never owned a service station.

Mr. Astoforoff: It was Peter Pankoff.[73]

This exchange went on for some time. Mr. Verigin, in questioning Mr. Astoforoff about the details of the meeting, wanted to know whether there was anyone present when the discussion took place in Pankoff's garage. Mr. Astoforoff replied that Peter Pankoff was present. Mr. Verigin then asked how close Mr. Pankoff had been to where they were having this discussion. Mr. Astoforoff, recognizing where Mr. Verigin was heading with his question, replied that Mr. Pankoff would not have known what they were talking about because both he (Mr. Astoforoff) and Mr. Verigin had been drinking for quite a while and were speaking in riddles. He added, "You don't give instructions when you're sober because you don't have an excuse."[74] Mr. Verigin abruptly ended his line of questioning. "Well, for the record, Mr. Astoforoff, the Court, having heard your testimony, disregarded it and as a result thereof, I was found not guilty of your allegations."[75]

Jim Popoff[76] asked Peter Astoforoff whether, given the inebriated condition of both men, he might have misunderstood the instructions that Mr. Verigin allegedly gave him. Mr. Astoforoff replied, "It's kind of late to ask that question now, Jim, because if I went ahead and went through with it, I must have stopped to think about it and looked at the possibility as to whether I had my head straight or not."[77]

Mr. Astoforoff's exchange with Mr. Verigin and Jim Popoff segued into a questioning of the role of USCC intermediaries, in particular that of Harry Voykin[78] and Joe Podovinikoff,[79] who had arranged meetings with the Sons of Freedom in early 1980. The committee learned that most of the meetings took place at the CEC Restaurant, which was operated by Harry Voykin and which was located next to the Doukhobor Museum in Ootischenia. The Sons of Freedom who attended the meetings wanted to know what role Mr. Voykin had been playing when he gave them what they considered to be "instructions" to burn or bomb. Peter Astoforoff told one such story about Sam Shlakoff, a Sons of Freedom member, who was one of the people to whom Harry Voykin had sent a message requesting a meeting at his restaurant.[80] Although Peter Astoforoff told the story, the story was about Sam Shlakoff, who was sitting nearby:

> This is the information I got from Sam. He says, "I wonder what the hell is going on with that Harry or his head, because he keeps asking for Hremakin. I bring Hremakin there. He sits there looking at him and he doesn't ask him any questions." He says, "We leave. And then the next few days, [Harry asks us to] bring Hremakin. So, I bring Hremakin and nothing happens, he just sits there looking at Hremakin. What is going on?" So, we start looking into this mystery, as we call it, and it turns out that Hremakin has another meaning in Russian, *hremet* [phonetic], to make noise. And also, Hremakin means that he is the person that is associated with dynamite, because this is what his role was amongst the Doukhobors. So, we had to come to a conclusion, when he asked for Hremakin and Hremakin is there and he won't ask him no questions and that next day he's phoning again, "Sam, bring Hremakin." So, it was the other Hremakin that he wanted and this is what our people around Gilpin understood that this was the Hremakin you were asking for all the time.[81]

Harry Voykin, who was also present in the room, was no clearer in his response. He said he had neither phoned Hremakin nor spoken to him while he was in his restaurant. He claimed that he did not talk to him because Hremakin might have been up to something. "Did you ever feel that it was your role in your community to kind of keep things stirred up and going?" asked Mr. Astoforoff. "Never, never. I have enough problems looking after myself, and my own, without looking after others," he replied.[82]

As bewildering as was the Hremakin story, Fred Makortoff, in summarizing what he had heard, said that it was becoming more and more evident that there was an official view behind which were unofficial activities. He added that this was not new information as many of the old Sons of Freedom had already described how the whole Doukhobor structure had been assembled, starting with Lordly, then Chistiakov, and continuing with John Verigin. He said he had no reason not to believe them as he had known them most of his life: "Now, either they're lying or their heads are scrambled ... [and] one of the best ways to get their heads unscrambled is to have this thing out in the open."[83] Mr. Makortoff said it was difficult to believe that the entire group of Sons of Freedom people, generation after generation, "could keep this boiling all by themselves, without some emphasis or reinforcement from outside" – a clear reference to the Orthodox leadership.[84]

Surprisingly, Mr. Verigin was in general agreement with Mr. Makortoff. Without explaining why and without elaborating upon any of the particulars, he shifted the discussion to the notion that it was time to sign a declaration to put an end to bombing and burning, which I saw more as a diversion than as a segue into a discussion of declarations. Mr. Makortoff made the point that, "for those like Peter Astoforoff's mother, who is throwing up blood right now and on her death bed, we will have a hell of a time trying to convince her that there weren't messages."[85] Peter Astoforoff made it clear that his perception of his leader could not simply change overnight: "To a person less evolved spiritually, [John Verigin] may be saying one thing and then another to another person that is aspiring for other things in life, the same speech could mean something else. What I am trying to say is that you get different meanings out of the same text."[86] He added that "each leader happens to have an agent or a middle man, such as I was," pointing out that this was so that the leadership would not be directly implicated. As a solution to this, he proposed that "the only thing they have to do is quit being agents or sending out messages."[87]

Speeches of Peter P. Verigin

Jack McIntosh, who served as Russian translator for the KCIR, found at UBC a number of speeches by Peter P. Verigin (Chistiakov), which he introduced as part of his KCIR presentation. He indicated that John Verigin had referred to a collection of speeches that Chistiakov wanted preserved, with the remainder to be purged from the file. Mr. McIntosh thought that ignoring speeches simply because they were no longer to be included as part of the collection raised many questions, especially when it came to understanding Chistiakov's role with the Sons of Freedom. As an example, he read from notes taken from a speech dated 27 January 1929 and presented by Peter P. Verigin in the village of Brilliant:

The speech began on the topic of the Freedomites: "behold our Freedomites. They are the rousing bells which will wake us up. Not the bells that ring and can be hear [sic] only around a church, but cannot be hear

[sic] further away. The Freedomites ring out so that they are heard for thousands of miles. Listen, this spring, we shall send out the young people to preach. They will ring out to the whole world. Even bones, which lay in the grave for a thousand years will shudder in the ground. The Freedomites are the head with the horns, the farmers the tail and the Community [Doukhobors], the Community people the belly filled with filth. The Freedomites are thirty-five years old; such the master can trust. He can put them onto a binder, place the reins in their hands and they can work. But Orthodox Doukhobors are fifteen years old and the farmers only three. The master cannot entrust a binder to such people because they have not grown up. They may let go of the reins, wreck the binder and kill themselves. The Freedomites are worthy."[88]

... At the end of the speech "Chistiakov unleashed thunder and lightening from his lips and began to feed the Freedomites with solid food, i.e., began to heap vulgar abuse upon them. Many were horrified and backed away from the Freedomite idea."[89]

John Verigin's reaction to Mr. McIntosh's presentation caught many of those present by surprise. In what was clearly an angry tone, he first wanted to know what Mr. McIntosh's role was on the EKCIR (even though Mr. McIntosh had been on the committee for some time), at which point the chair, Robin Bourne, intervened to explain. Mr. Verigin reiterated that Peter P. Verigin had "selected speeches and letters that were to serve as guidelines for future generations." "I do not believe that Mr. Chistiakov had two different policies, one for the government and another for his close ... or intimate or followers," he said.[90] Robin Bourne wondered what effect Mr. Verigin's removing the speech from Peter P. Verigin's collection (thus implying that it had never existed) might have had on someone like Mr. Nevokshonoff,[91] who had been present at the time the speech had been delivered.

Jim Popoff suggested that, if one were to study all of Peter P. Verigin's speeches and other recommended writings, then one would see a consistent ideological pattern throughout: "You cannot talk about a double meaning because his words had a single meaning for him."[92] Peter Astoforoff argued that Chistiakov states in the Brilliant speech that some have been trained to see "different meanings, in accordance to [one's] level of spiritual development," adding: "it is obvious why this speech is not one of the selected speeches because the selected speeches were intended for fifteen-year-olds."[93] This clearly implies that the speeches intended for the Sons of Freedom were the ones that were purged from the collection.

This exchange illustrates how important it was for the USCC to maintain a certain narrative consistency. What is not accounted for in Peter Verigin's story is the underlying message that the Sons of Freedom held on to for their own purposes – whether spiritual, political, or otherwise – and that justified the years of destruction. Jim Popoff concluded that history clearly shows that the Sons of Freedom systematically misinterpreted what Chistiakov had said, even though he chose his words carefully. Mr. Popoff acknowledged that he accepted the possibility that the Sons of Freedom may have interpreted his words on a symbolic level, adding that a misinterpretation of a single sentence or a simple act had led to the deaths of thousands in countries like the Soviet Union: "We cannot turn back all the pages of history and we cannot definitely ever define what was inside Mr. Verigin's mind."[94]

The first USCC witness to appear at the 4 October 1983 session was Peter Popoff, the former head of the Doukhobor Research Committee, a group that had formed in the mid-1970s to document Doukhobor experiences. Mr. Popoff read a statement that indicated that the research committee members, who were mainly Orthodox and some of whom were present at the EKCIR sessions (along with a few Independent Doukhobors), were deeply disturbed by presentations made to the EKCIR by members of the Sons of Freedom and Reformed Doukhobors:

> We are very disturbed mainly because the two above mentioned groups persist in their intentions of involving, by fabricated and twisted evidence as found from their presentation at the symposium, innocent people including the traditional Doukhobor Spiritual Leaders. Their concerted attempts to shed responsibility for their own acts by making it appear someone else is responsible, has caused great concern to many. This conspiracy has caused a serious division inside the over-all Doukhobor society, with a terrific financial burden on many. But to the USCC especially, in matters of security, insurance, property, etceteras, not to mention the adverse publicity and the denigration of the Doukhobor public image.[95]

Peter Popoff added that there were two instances in which fire was used publicly, with the approval of the Orthodox members. The first occurred in Russia in 1895 at the "burning of the arms," and the second occurred in the 1920s in Verigin, Saskatchewan, when firearms owned by many Independent Doukhobors were destroyed at a Peter's Day observance. He claimed that at no other time was the community involved in setting fires. Peter Popoff said that the Doukhobor Symposia[96] found no evidence of any instruction or justification for destroying other people's property or for causing other people to suffer. In support of his findings he cited numerous examples from speeches given both by Peter the Lordly and Peter Chistiakov. He concluded by saying, "No one has accepted this challenge to prove that arson, violence and destruction of other people's property are part of the Doukhobor faith and philosophy and no one was able to disprove the facts cited above."[97]

Strategically, the USCC needed to find a way to bring the EKCIR back to what was essentially the dominant Orthodox story. I assumed that the USCC was feeling pressured by those not participating in the sessions but who were hearing stories about what was being said there. One can also assume that many Orthodox and Independent Doukhobors who were not in attendance might have been wondering why it was that the Sons of Freedom and Reformed stories were being given any consideration at all.

Following Peter Popoff's presentation, Peter Astoforoff asked, "Do I understand you correctly to mean that some of your people are starting to doubt or starting to believe that perhaps maybe orders did come from leaders?"

> Mr. Popoff: Well, that's what is being said and that's why this presentation.
> Mr. Astoforoff: Okay. Further, you state that you cannot find the documented proof that leaders gave orders or something to that effect. Is that correct?
> Mr. Popoff: That is correct.

Mr. Astoforoff pressed Mr. Popoff regarding what he meant by "documented proof," asking whether his own statement, which he gave in court and in which he said that he received instructions from John Verigin, would qualify as "documented proof." Peter Popoff said that his comment was referring to former Verigin leaders – in particular, to Peter Petrovich Verigin – rather than to John Verigin.

Mr. Makortoff asked Peter Popoff why the Doukhobor Research Committee rejected a presentation by Nick Nevokshonoff, noting that he was a trustworthy man and that the purpose of the research committee was to examine Doukhobor history. "Why was he not allowed, if you were after the truth?" Mr. Makortoff asked. Peter Popoff, who chaired the Doukhobor Research Symposia, explained that Mr. Nevokshonoff's presentation would have aroused a lot of hostility among the members. Mr. Makortoff responded, "there was nothing vulgar ... about it ... he even refrained from mentioning the names of the people involved so as to avoid any unpleasantness to their grandchildren."[98] "As you probably are aware ... we have a rule for the symposiums that unsubstantiated accusations of any person, dead or alive, [are] not acceptable. And this is what he was trying to do," Mr. Popoff replied.

It was apparent that the Doukhobor Research Committee had attempted to maintain a certain story-line regarding Doukhobor history. Denying the possibility that other stories might be valid, it further marginalized the other groups, which, in the end, left the Sons of Freedom and Reformed Doukhobors more determined than ever to counter these views through other means.

Negotiating Stephan Sorokin's Participation

By the October 1983 EKCIR session, Stephan Sorokin had returned from Montevideo, Uruguay, where he had lived off and on since the early 1950s. Prior to the October session the Sons of Freedom had erected a tent village on empty land across the road from the Castlegar airport to serve as a protest camp for those who were demanding Mr. Sorokin's participation at the EKCIR sessions. I met with the Sons of Freedom at the protest site to see whether there was anything I could do to assist in bringing this matter to an end. After having spent the better part of an hour with those at the camp, I went to see Stephan Sorokin and members of the Reformed Doukhobors to discuss with them the Sons of Freedom concerns. Mr. Sorokin and his close confidants spent a good part of the time discussing the motives of certain people, recalling that, prior to his departure for Uruguay, Sons of Freedom members had attacked his residence. The question being discussed was whether Mr. Sorokin's refusal to attend the sessions would provide the Sons of Freedom and the USCC with further fodder to attack his credibility. Although his health was poor, he indicated that he would attend, and I returned to the camp to inform people of his answer.

I sat with the Sons of Freedom in their tent, listening to various people discuss Mr. Sorokin's reply. There were between thirty and forty people present. It was late in the day, and, as dusk set in, the tent became darker and darker until I could barely make out who was speaking. After they talked for a while they asked if they could deliver their answer to me at my hotel later in the evening. I agreed and left. About midnight I noticed a piece of paper under my door indicating their response. In short, they agreed to end their protest.

The next day I noticed that the Sons of Freedom seemed sad as they went about their business of removing the camp. My impression was that the protest camp had brought them together for the first time in many years for a common purpose, and that there was something about this that they didn't want to lose.

Stephan Sorokin – The Hawk

The session with Stephan Sorokin started off rather unevenly as it was difficult to coordinate the Russian/English translations with Mr. Sorokin, who was not used to the proceedings. Before the meeting he was provided with a list of questions, some focusing on his identity as *Yastrebov* (the Hawk) – a name that he either was given or had assumed, depending on whom you asked – and the impression it created for many Doukhobor and Sons of Freedom people.[99] Mr. Sorokin explained that when he arrived in the Kootenays John Lebedoff[100] had taken advantage of the occasion by bringing him to the Sons of Freedom and introducing him as their long lost leader. According to Mr. Sorokin, "Lebedoff was behind all the terrorism from Verigin. Here, I immediately took action so he [Lebedoff] would be vanished from Krestova and then he was put in jail."[101]

The symbolism of the "hawk" was very important among all the Doukhobors as it stood for the long lost leader Peter Verigin the Third, who was living in the Soviet Union and who was considered to be next in line to Peter Petrovich as leader of the Doukhobors. The USCC was concerned that Mr. Sorokin was exploiting the situation by taking advantage of the Sons of Freedom by pretending that he was Peter Verigin the Third. Much of the exchange between Mr. Sorokin and the USCC concerned this matter.

Other Sons of Freedom Leaders

John Lebedoff, another prominent Sons of Freedom "leader" during the 1940s, decided to make an appearance at the EKCIR sessions. In his former role he was viewed as an intermediary between the Verigin leadership and the Sons of Freedom and, as mentioned above, he was the one who, in 1950, introduced Mr. Sorokin to the Sons of Freedom as the long lost leader *Yastrebov*. When he appeared as a witness he read a statement denying any involvement in burnings and arson – a statement that was contrary to the views of those who were with him during the period in question. Many were looking forward to insights he might provide into his role during that time; however, he did little to help anyone understand why the fires continued as they had. This was a disappointment for many.

Mike Bayoff was also a self-proclaimed leader within the Sons of Freedom movement. He was a tall man with long white hair, who wore mainly white and who always carried a collection of papers that he was ready to present whenever called upon. During the sessions he sat as an "independent" Sons of Freedom. Other than occasionally asking people to speak more loudly, he sat quietly waiting for his opportunity to present.

The ad hoc planning Committee, which was made up of representatives from the Doukhobor groups, myself, and members of the KCIR core group, finally agreed that Mr. Bayoff could make his presentation at the January 1984 session. His entire presentation consisted of reading numerous pages from Simma Holt's *Terror in the Name of God*, which described how he assisted the police in unravelling the secrecy surrounding the numerous bombings that had taken place during the 1950s and 1960s. He offered no new insights.

Conclusion

The sessions began with the USCC making it known that it was a law-abiding group that had endured years of victimization at the hands of the "terrorists" and, when John Verigin was arrested, had suffered further victimization at the hands of the justice system. For them, being victims meant that they had to endure the loss of buildings destroyed by fire (along with the additional costs of insuring and guarding their properties) as well as being stigmatized by the unfair belief that all Doukhobors were burners and bombers.

The Sons of Freedom also endured the loss of their homes through fire, albeit at times by choice. For those who spent time in jail, many lost their health (through fasting) and their families (through years of incarceration). The role of the Sons of Freedom, however conceived, was part of a complex web of beliefs, oblique messages, "black work" (covert protest activities), secrets, salvation, sacrifice, intimidation, and fear. Although all of the parties longed for an end to the years of turmoil, no one was willing either to compromise their beliefs or to discontinue their activities until change was evident. For the USCC, change meant no more guarding, rebuilding, or paying high insurance costs. For the Sons of Freedom, change meant being emancipated from the religious/cultural burden they saw themselves as bearing.

Bringing the groups together meant finding the right person to chair the process. Robin Bourne personified this role as he was, first, an outsider to the area, which seemed to have its own cachet; second, he was a senior bureaucrat in the provincial government and had had a prior history in Soviet affairs;[102] and third, he was someone who had demonstrated an interest in helping to address the long-standing issues between the Doukhobor groups and the provincial government.

The success of the first EKCIR session was due in part to the groups' having input into designing the rules of engagement. However, another important factor was Robin Bourne's role in maintaining decorum and ensuring that those who were willing to speak about their experiences did so while knowing what to expect.

In the beginning, my role was to shuttle back and forth between the Doukhobor groups until an agreement was reached on the structure and rules of engagement. After the first session, once the groups were committed to continuing, I spent my time addressing matters that arose, which included intervening in hunger fasts, mitigating conflicts, and/ or looking through archival sources in Victoria and Ottawa.

5
Negotiating a New Narrative

Since the first EKCIR session John Verigin had, on a number of occasions, proposed that everyone sign a declaration to end the bombings and arson. Such a declaration would be one of faith rather than one resulting from an answer to the question of why the turmoil had continued for so long. The question some were asking was this: if they were to agree to sign a declaration, would this be perceived as an endorsement of Mr. Verigin's leadership? And, if so, would this result in a dismissal of whatever past role and influence the Verigins might have had on the Sons of Freedom? The challenge for the Doukhobor groups concerned deciding whether to accept such a proposal on faith or whether to continue listening to the testimony of those who had been involved.

It was during the 2 May 1984 session, when Fred Makortoff asked John Verigin if he remembered meeting with W.A.C. Bennett in 1972 in Grand Forks, that Mr. Verigin indicated he could furnish fifty names of people who were insane and fifty names of hardened criminals. Mr. Verigin said "that the record would indicate ... those who were involved in these acts ... can be identified ... through [a] doctor's observation ... whether they should be considered as criminals or ... need medical attention."[1] He indicated that he believed that providing such a list would make it easier for the police and the community to know who should be watched. At this point the tension in the room became noticeable.

John Ostricoff, a Reformed Doukhobor, reminded Mr. Verigin that he was asking everyone to forget the past. "How can you forget the past if you are looked on as either mentally insane or a criminal who should be put away"?[2] Jim Popoff intervened to say that if they were to reach a reconciliation then there would no longer be a need for such a list. However, this increased rather than lessened the tension in the room. John Ostricoff, now notably angry, stated, "The USCC members [are] denying the fact that these principles were mutual principles. You're

[also] denying the fact that these [Sons of Freedom] were the front army people that went out and defended these principles." "Why," he asked, "is the USCC denying its role"[3]?

Jim Popoff explained that there were 30,000 people of Doukhobor background in Canada and that less than 1 percent might agree with Mr. Ostricoff's theory that bombing and burning was a legitimate front-line activity. "I don't agree with it and I don't see why I have to buy that theory before you will be willing to stop burning and bombing," he said. "The reason for all the bombing and arson was because the principles, such as not buying land, were those of Chistiakov," Mr. Ostricoff argued, "and these principles were instigated by these leaders, through his front army people here that went out and fought for their lives towards that and lost their wives and kids and everything else."[4]

Jim Popoff, in an attempt to diffuse the situation, commented that "no one abides by principles perfectly," adding that the breaking of principles (in regard to the land, etc.) was not a justification for burning and bombing. Returning to the point, John Ostricoff argued that the USCC was using their majority argument as their defence:

> You built yourself a shield, you've used it and now you're turning back in another sense and accusing us, because we cannot accuse you, because we're uneducated. You didn't send us to school and things like that, they were prohibited, otherwise Peter the Lordly's blood would fall upon us with such fear. We grew up with such fear like this to understand this. And here you say that there was no such a thing taking place like that.[5]

Fred Makortoff said that, after two years of hearing witnesses, it was clear that the USCC was not willing to acknowledge the Sons of Freedom's role. And he observed that, over the past few months, a rage was starting to build among Sons of Freedom members. He again explained that the Sons of Freedom were "the vanguard, the ringing bells, the guys that made noises far, far away. We were the guys that did this, sacrificed many things ... it takes a lot of jam to go and do something like that and have a whole pile of misfortune staring you in the face and still go and do it."[6] He added that everyone was promised that someday there would be an accounting of all that had happened. In other words, people were told that there was a grand scheme behind all the bombings and burnings.

The underlying issue for Jim Popoff was the "false stigmatization of the true Doukhobor ideology ... [This was] where we have to listen to the TV and hear about Doukhobor violence when violence has nothing to do with Doukhoborism." He added that "it takes a lot of jam to take all that shit and still say: Look man, let's get together and be human beings together and let's not hurt each other."[7]

After a lengthy exchange, Chair Robin Bourne recapitulated the main points, saying that the Sons of Freedom believed that they were being clearly directed by the Verigin leadership and that they were expected to burn and bomb in the interest of upholding Doukhobor principles. Mr. Bourne turned to John Verigin at this point: "What you're being asked to admit, Mr. Verigin, is the responsibility of the Doukhobor leadership for the direction, either obliquely or directly, for the actions ... taken by the Sons of Freedom."[8] Robin Bourne knew that the USCC was adamant that they had never counselled either burnings or bombings. However, he also knew that the opportunity for reaching an accord would rest on Mr. Verigin's acknowledgment of the Sons of Freedom role. The pressure was clearly on Mr. Verigin to decide how far he would go to construct a new narrative that would include, rather than ex-clude, the Sons of Freedom. Clearly, his preference was to ignore the Sons of Freedom and simply have everyone sign a declaration to end the bombing and arson. Mr. Bourne in his attempt to deconstruct Mr. Verigin's logic, said:

> You're condemning the Sons of Freedom to their own responsibility for these acts forevermore. And I don't think that's acceptable to them. I think the Reformed who call themselves Reformed because they have pledged not to take part in violent activities, but a great many of them did take part in violent activities when they were Sons of Freedom, also feel that unless their perceptions that these activities, going back to the early days, were in part anyway, the responsibility of the leadership, that they also will be condemned [for] having taken part in violence.[9]

Robin Bourne concluded that he was not suggesting that Mr. Verigin was guilty of anything but, rather, that if he wanted to end the burnings and bombings then he would have to "do the right thing" and acknowl-edge the past role of the Sons of Freedom. This was the only way to move beyond the present impasse.

Jim Popoff said that he had already acknowledged that the Sons of Freedom had suffered more than had the USCC. However, his com-ments quickly went sideways when he suggested that their suffering came about because of their "perceived beliefs."[10] Fred Makortoff quickly challenged Jim Popoff on his use of the phrase "perceived beliefs": "[This] sort of puts the onus on the person that saw this erroneously. That there was something wrong with the guy's head and he sees with square eye-balls or something, I don't know."[11] Mr. Makortoff reminded everyone that, over time, the Doukhobors had developed an "oblique language." The Sons of Freedom knew what this language meant and where it came from. As for their "perceived beliefs," Mr. Makortoff pointed out that people had long ago learned that they should verify a message if they had any doubt about it. He added that it was easy to talk about the past, forgetting that what was being left out of the discussion were people's emotions:

> They don't have the capacity to manipulate words easily, they feel frus-trated. Doukhobors are a peculiar kind of people. They can sit in the meeting hall there, where we had people sitting on the same bench where one guy made a statement on the next guy and he's done five years in the slammer for it. The guy was completely innocent, he was never there. The guy did it to save him so that he could go to the mother Russia, see. And both of these guys are sitting on the same bench sing-ing praises to the Lord. It's difficult to find that in other societies.[12]

Robin Bourne saw the opportunity to again ask Mr. Verigin if he had given any further thought, "as the current member of the Verigin lead-ership, to acknowledge any responsibility or blame for the depredations that were caused by the Sons of Freedom. I'm not asking you person-ally, but I'm asking you whether the history of the Verigin leadership is prepared, through you, to acknowledge that they bear responsibility for some of these acts."[13] John Verigin replied:

> I'd be admitting to a falsehood. The true facts as I know, being a living example of the so-called Verigin leadership, if I am regarded as such, is to this; I swear before you as before God, never have I given any in-structions to anybody and in that manner to say that I have been re-sponsible for a commission of an act that was committed by somebody who chose to misinterpret me, would be tantamount to give credence, credibility to these actions ... what I'm seeking is this – I want to assure everybody present that today and tomorrow, nobody has to fear that there will be any instructions, directly or indirectly, verbally, writtenly [sic], orally, to commit such actions.[14]

Although the day ended on a positive note, over the next five months the relationship among the Doukhobor groups soured. During this time the pressure remained on John Verigin and the USCC to acknowledge that Chistiakov had encouraged the Sons of Freedom in their activities.

At the planning committee meeting on 18 June, Peter Astoforoff said that the Sons of Freedom were not going to support any proposal in which they looked like "Mr. Black" while other groups looked like "Mr. Clean."[15] Mr. Astoforoff's position was that the Orthodox Doukhobors needed to accept that Chistiakov and John Verigin conveyed to some people information that led to certain "acts." John Verigin asked how he could approach an average USCC member, especially one who had spent time guarding property or had helped pay for the reconstruction of the USCC centre, and ask them to accept reasonable blame for what had happened. Peter Astoforoff acknowledged that this would be very difficult for John Verigin; however, the Sons of Freedom would not make any kind of commitment until somebody shared responsibility for the so-called "black work."

At the 8 August planning committee meeting, Peter Astoforoff again repeated that the problem was that everyone was too concerned about having a clean image while at the same time disowning those who were responsible for unacceptable acts. He suggested that the groups quit blaming each other and try to look at the problem objectively. He characterized the acts of depredation as a "form of zeal" that erupted spontaneously, and he suggested that people needed to understand how to control this zeal so that it did not erupt into more violent acts. The debate continued late into the evening.[16] At the 10 September planning committee meeting this "zeal" reached fever pitch when Mr. Verigin arrived inebriated, leaving the KCIR members wondering whether continuing with the process was worth their time.

The next EKCIR session, held in October 1983, began on a low note. In his opening comments Chair Robin Bourne stated that, since the past eight sessions had produced no tangible result, he was proposing three options for everyone to consider: the first was to end the proceedings and let people go back to what they were doing; the second was to have he and I replaced with another provincial government representative; and the third was to design a new project that would not involve the provincial government but, rather, would leave the discussions to local people. While everyone considered his comments, the KCIR members made their presentation. This began with a letter written to Peter Makaroff, QC, who served as legal counsel to the Doukhobor community. The letter was written by W.A. Soukeroff on 14 March 1962, and it stated:

Verigin Sr. [Peter V. Verigin] definitely pursued a policy opposed to as-similation. No matter what people say, we are all witnesses to the fact that he was afraid that, having provided education to his flock, he would either lose them or it would facilitate normal assimilation of the Doukhobors with his life around them. To his methods the Freedomites added their stubbornness, and were merely upholding ancient behest and aspirations.

Even if he did not give his blessing to terrorism, Peter Petrovich ut-tered very much what was unclear to the people and forced them to conjecture. His favorite analogy had to do with cleaning potatoes, as he put it; "I will clean them and feed the skins to the pigs." Another analogy was the example he would always cite of the hen under which most of the eggs were spoiled and he was compelling the chicks to peck their way out so as not to die in the shell. He also established the fre-quency of Doukhobor migrations, defining it to be every 40 years, and insisted that the Doukhobors had outlived their stay in Canada, and must take action; the first step – breakfast – was the rejection of the church and icons, the second – dinner – was the burning of arms. The third step, he declared would be taken in Canada, and would be the final supper, but he did not say clearly what specifically had to be done.

And so, all of these obscure sayings, given the Freedomites' naïve faith, even unto death and loss of self, and their zeal to see to it that his words, which they now call "prophesies," were not in vain, have com-pelled the Freedomites to offer themselves as scapegoats, by means of burnings and bombings goading the government into expelling them from Canada, thereby providing a reason, as they put it: "we won't leave without a reason."[17]

Other prominent Doukhobors who had kept a watchful eye on the situation over the years offered presentations. One was from P.K. Reiben who, at the time, was the representative of the Independent Doukhobors within the Union of Doukhobors of Canada. On 15 August 1947 he wrote an "open letter" to the Union of Doukhobors of Canada in which he made a number of claims, one of which suggested that the disinte-gration of Doukhobor society was the result of how that society was structured. He believed that this led to unbearably oppressive condi-tions within Doukhobor communal life and to the "unbridled despot-ism of the leaders and their henchmen."[18] Reiben claimed that "almost all the entourage of former leaders were themselves involved in this black work, and hence, fearing [for] their own skin, they have zealously concealed this secret."[19]

Jim Kolesnikoff, a USCC member who had remained quiet throughout most of the EKCIR sessions, thought it was conceivable that the Doukhobors did behave in a very erratic and inexplicable manner. He said that it would be beneficial for the Doukhobors to understand some of the "deep rooted causes for this behavior."[20] He cited examples taken from archival materials that had not been previously available. I was concerned that this discussion was now heading in a new direction without having finished what had been started. My sense at the time was that, whenever an issue came close to being resolved, the discussion would either suddenly turn to some other issue or end in a series of personal attacks. I reminded everyone that we were addressing perspectives, not looking for causes, and I suggested that we finish discussing the role of Chistiakov before moving to another topic. Everyone agreed.

Robin Bourne took this opportunity to revisit the question of whether the Orthodox Doukhobors were prepared to acknowledge that some of Chistiakov's statements and actions might have been "misinterpreted," leading some to believe that bombings and burnings did indeed have their place. John Verigin replied that "Chistiakov and even Lordly could have been misinterpreted or contributed to a development of a certain kind"[21]; however, he added that both had been dead for some time and that he himself has been accused of making similar statements. He challenged anyone to attribute responsibility to him. The chair again asked Mr. Verigin if he was prepared to admit that some of his statements (and actions) could have been misinterpreted. Mr. Verigin replied: "I would like to know exactly what statement and where could there be possibly a misrepresentation, because the basic issue, burnings and bombings, I have always stated – they are not compatible with the Doukhobor principles of faith. I have always stated openly that, I don't believe anyone that says that he's got instructions from me to do this. And I challenge anyone to prove otherwise."[22]

Mel Stangeland, a KCIR member, decided it was time to respond to Mr. Verigin's challenge by referring to a planning committee meeting of 10 September 1984 that had left the KCIR members wondering whether what they were doing was worth the effort. This was a meeting that had been chaired by Mr. Stangeland and at which a number of Sons of Freedom, Reformed, and Orthodox Doukhobors were present. Mr. Stangeland reported that Mr. Verigin arrived at the meeting intoxicated and that, from the moment he arrived, had been disorderly and difficult to manage. When John Verigin did speak, Mr. Stangeland added, he spoke in Russian to the Sons of Freedom, which led Mary Astoforoff to stand up and set fire to a twenty-dollar bill. When she finished burning the money, she disrobed. At this point Mr. Gritchin, who drove Mr. Verigin to the meeting, offered to take him home. "On his way out of the hall, [Mr. Verigin] made a point of going over to Mrs. Astoforoff and standing quite close to her and spoke to her in Russian, and then turned around and shook hands with Mr. Savinkoff – Peter Savinkoff, who is a self-confessed arsonist – who had burned down the community center in Grand Forks. And those were the only two people that he made any kind of statement to or gave any real attention to on his way out of the hall."[23] Mr. Stangeland concluded by saying, "if a person is really concerned about not creating misunderstandings and confusion, those are not the kinds of actions that are going to contribute to peace in the Kootenays."[24] Mr. Verigin responded:

> Mr. Stangeland, at one point you say that I was an intoxicated person. Then I would say then if that is an illustration to take into account, maybe that explains why in my eyes at that particular moment I only saw Mrs. Astoforoff and this Peter Savinkoff. Would that not be a human explanation for my behavior?[25]

Mr. Stangeland said he wasn't looking for an explanation but simply pointing out what he and others saw. This was "an open and friendly discussion between you and two Sons of Freedom, one of whom had just disrobed and burned the money in the presence of the meeting."[26]

Following this exchange, the KCIR resumed its presentation. I read a letter addressed to the Honourable Hugh Guthrie, KC, minister of justice in Ottawa, from the attorney general of British Columbia, the Honourable R.H. Pooley. The letter was dated 17 January 1932.

> There can be no doubt in the world that Peter [P.] Verigin knows exactly what is going on and from what Secret Service people tell us, he is fully advised as to contemplated actions. The files of the RCMP would illustrate to you that our information is of an authentic nature, because it was our police who learned that it was the intention of the Doukhobors to destroy property in Saskatchewan and blow up some of the elevators. The RCMP were immediately advised by wire and they were able to frustrate the contemplated dynamiting, which was planned to take place within forty-eight hours. And now we are advised of the intention to destroy several more schools ... I want to impress upon you – subject to what the members of the RCMP may think – our view is that the situation would be very much improved if an ultimatum should be

delivered to Peter P. Verigin, that if these outrages are not stopped he will be deported. Let me remind you that Peter Verigin was the man who stated at a Doukhobor gathering that bridges would be blown up, and we all know that several attempts have been made to do that very thing since he made that statement.[27]

The RCMP pursued the matter further. Eventually an aborted attempt was made to have Peter Petrovich Verigin deported back to the Soviet Union.

I also read from an RCMP report that referred to a "Special Agent 878," who was spending time with both Peter P. Verigin (as a translator) and two Sons of Freedom leaders named Peter N. Maloff and John Perepelkin. In a meeting that the agent attended with John Perepelkin, he (the agent) learned that the Sons of Freedom were becoming agitated because they heard that Peter P. Verigin was going to remove them from their lands in order to create a clear separation between them and the Orthodox Doukhobors. This information resulted in many Sons of Freedom homes being set ablaze and an irrigation pipe being dynamited. Special Agent 878 said in his report that those responsible were not Sons of Freedom but, rather, "Communal Doukhobors," which was the term applied to Orthodox Doukhobors. His information seemed to fit what some others claimed to already know.

The KCIR concluded its presentation in October 1984 by stating that if the parties were to move beyond the impasse then they needed to agree upon a joint statement that redefined Chistiakov's role. Surprisingly, everyone agreed. Mel Stangeland said that he and Mark Mealing had prepared a draft statement, based on a letter by W.A. Soukeroff, for the committee to consider. The statement described how the Sons of Freedom movement grew in numbers from 1927 to 1938 under the leadership of Peter P. Verigin and that, although Chistiakov did not publicly advocate terrorism, his sayings, parables, and speeches created such confusion in the minds of the people that some of his utterances served as the foundation for acts of violence.

The groups decided they would review the draft over lunch. Later, when the session resumed, each group acknowledged that the draft statement "safely" described this period without offending any of the groups in particular. John Verigin proposed some changes, which led to a discussion over the appropriateness of certain words. When it became clear that a new draft was needed in order to reflect the changes, the groups agreed that Mel Stangeland and Mark Mealing should be left to work on it while the Sons of Freedom made their presentation.

The Sons of Freedom presentation stood in sharp contrast to the previous discussion about Chistiakov's role. It was as though the previous discussion had not even occurred. Accusations and counter-accusations were once again being made, this time concerning Stephan Sorokin's role and how Mary Malakoff had been assaulted, presumably by the Reformed Doukhobors. In the midst of this melee, Jim Popoff and John Verigin proposed an "interim draft reconciliation pledge." Jim Popoff explained that the USCC executive was putting pressure on Mr. Verigin and his delegates to account for the time they had been spending at these sessions over the past two years. The chair asked that the document be set aside for discussion on the last day. This meant that two initiatives were now under way – the Chistiakov statement and the Orthodox proposal for reconciliation.

Crafting Language and Meaning

Mel Stangeland and Mark Mealing presented their new draft of the statement describing Chistiakov's role, at which point negotiation over the wording of the document began. Notably absent during this exchange were any accusations or counter-accusations. It was as though two years of intense wrangling over beliefs, positions, and accusations had been for naught. The careful crafting of language continued on into the evening, until finally:

> Dr. Mealing: 1. The Freedomite movement grew rapidly in the years 1927-1938, during the leadership of Peter P. Verigin. The Sons of Freedom arose within the Doukhobor community and yearned for a leader whose role, purpose, methods and values would satisfy their radical hopes.
>
> 2. Peter P. Verigin did not publicly advocate terrorism.
>
> 3. Peter P. Verigin commonly used sayings, parables and teachings that created confusion in the minds of people, including Doukhobors, Government Officials and Police and this allowed them to construct their own interpretations. Some of these interpretations remain to the present day a foundation for acts of violence.
>
> 4. Leaders and members of all Doukhobor groups shared antipathy to Government, a common concern about principles or ownership, and fear of assimilation and the loss of Doukhobor principles.
>
> 5. Factionalization grew because of the various degrees to which individual Doukhobors were willing to act in this common struggle. 7.
>
> Mr. Verigin: 6.

Dr. Mealing: That's right. I can count, but not this late at night – 6. We, representatives of the Christian Community and Brotherhood of Reformed Doukhobors, of the Sons of Freedom, and of the Union of Spiritual Communities of Christ –
Mr. Bourne: The meeting is adjourned. Let's shake hands.[28]

Fred Makortoff started the next morning by offering his thoughts about the previous evening's session, which appeared to match what others felt as well.

I think yesterday has restored some confidence in the process for everybody. I think it has also indicated a wise choice of a way to proceed, this matter of focusing on an area. This focusing should be pursued and continued, in the hope of gaining more agreements as to events and the circumstances surrounding events. And in this way we can – there is enough background information over the last eight sessions, where everybody has a general idea of what is happening ... We're pleased with the agreement. There is a lot more that we would have liked to see, but in the interest of achieving some agreement, we're quite prepared to live with that.[29]

Those in the room felt a renewed confidence. Later in the day the chair brought back for discussion the "interim draft reconciliation pledge" that Jim Popoff had introduced the night before. In raising the "pledge" for discussion, the chair was hoping that the same approach introduced by Mel Stangeland and Mark Mealing might be adopted. In other words, even though this statement was a product of the USCC, the chair did not want to see the discussion reduced to personal attacks, as had happened on numerous other occasions. The draft statement began with a preamble that described the role of the individual Doukhobor in his/her service to his/her faith. The statement ended with a commitment to end bombings and burnings, recognizing that such acts have no role in the Doukhobor movement.

Although most felt the statement sounded conciliatory, there was a sense of caution about proceeding too far until there was time for the other groups to mull it over. Peter Astoforoff indicated that putting signatures on a piece of paper did not require much effort and that the challenge would be in living up to the words on the paper. The chair asked that I meet with the groups between sessions to find a way to craft an accord statement to end the bombings and arson that everyone could live with. He concluded by suggesting that the decision as to whether to continue with the EKCIR would be left to the attorney general, who would be given recommendations based on the advice from the groups and the progress that had been made at this session.

Negotiating an Accord

The next session wasn't until April 1985, so there was time for me to make my way back and forth between the Doukhobor groups to seek agreement. I used Robin Bourne's comments at the end of the October session as leverage.

When I met with the Reformed Doukhobors, I found that they felt the sessions had been valuable and wanted to see them continue. I raised with them the notion that an accord could speak to their desire to continue the process and, at the same time, include the type of "reconciliation" language that the Orthodox Doukhobors were proposing. They agreed.

The USCC also wanted to see the sessions continue; however, they needed to demonstrate to their membership that progress was being made. The Sons of Freedom, on the other hand, were ambivalent about signing any document. They were willing to give their word to end their participation in bombings and arson as long as they did not receive such instructions from the leaders.

There were a number of events that occurred during this six-month period, including the death of Stephan Sorokin, who died a month after the October 1984 session. Also, a week prior to the April 1985 session a bomb was discovered along the railroad tracks near Grand Forks, and two Sons of Freedom women were arrested for breach of parole after they set their home ablaze in Gilpin.

Signing the Interim Accord

During this period between EKCIR sessions I decided to meet with all of the parties individually to discuss the draft USCC reconciliation statement. The Reformed Doukhobors saw this as an opportunity to push the province to commit to the continuation of the EKCIR process and to see how committed Mr. Verigin was to ending the turmoil. They indicated that before they would sign the statement, John Verigin would need to sign a declaration stating that he would not instruct anyone to commit further acts of arson and bombing. I relayed this information to the Sons of Freedom in Gilpin and then to Mr. Verigin, Jim Popoff, and other members of his team.

The Sons of Freedom response was that they wanted to wait and see the final draft. When I introduced the terms proposed by the Reformed Doukhobors to the USCC, Mr. Verigin agreed – to the astonishment of his members – that he would sign a declaration. Jim Popoff volunteered to draft the declaration statement, which I then delivered to the Reformed Doukhobors. The Reformed were uneasy with the wording and so redrafted. I took this rewritten draft back to the USCC. After two more visits, the groups finally settled on the wording. I arranged a planning committee meeting for 19 February, which would be the first time since October that everyone would be in the same room.

At the planning committee meeting the groups seemed relieved that an agreement had been reached. This they saw as a historic occasion; although the question that I presumed was on everyone's mind was how long the agreement would hold. The language that they agreed to in the "Interim Accord" read:

We, the undersigned hereby state: (1) That we condemn any or all bombings and arson of the past, present and future; (2) That to the best of our ability we will try to deter those who still wish to continue in such acts of violence; and (3) That we promise to continue our participation in a co-operative process involving all three Doukhobor groups, namely, the USCC, the Sons of Freedom and the Christian Community of Reformed Doukhobors along with representatives from Government and the Kootenay Committee on Intergroup Relations so that every effort can be made to understand the reasons for the years of suffering in order to insure that the suffering along with the bitterness and strife, will not continue into the future.[30]

The declaration that Mr. Verigin signed read:

"I, John J. Verigin, honorary chairman of the Union of Spiritual Communities of Christ, hereby declare: (a) That I will not curse anybody to commit acts of violence; and (b) that I will not instruct or counsel anybody to commit criminal acts such as arson and bombings. I hereby sign this document in good faith." And it was signed and dated the 19th day of February 1985 at Castlegar, British Columbia.[31]

Although the Sons of Freedom members were kept informed throughout this process, in the end they chose not to sign. The reason, they indicated, was that they were withdrawing formally from the EKCIR because of threats they had received and a recent fire that had taken place at the residence of one of their members. They did, however, agree that they would abide by the spirit of the accord.

Jim Popoff wanted it stated for the record that curses had nothing to do with Doukhoborism.[32] He also stated that a previous draft of the declaration presented by the Reformed Doukhobors read: "I will not curse anybody to commit acts of violence as of now." Mr. Popoff pointed out that "as of now" implied that Mr. Verigin had cursed somebody in the past, whereas in the signed declaration the phrase had a line through it, indicating that the words were to be omitted, with the correction to be initialled when the document was signed. However, copies of the document had already circulated throughout the various communities. The problem was that in the circulated copies the "as of now" phrase was still visible and the change had not been noted. The conclusion was that the blue ink had not shown up on the photocopy, which did not sit easily with the Orthodox representatives. In their defence, the Reformed Doukhobors said that they had provided a copy to an Independent Doukhobor who took it upon himself to make additional copies to circulate among the communities. A debate ensued until the chair reminded everyone that progress had been made.

Conclusion

After two years of ongoing EKCIR sessions it was now evident that the previously dominant narratives no longer had a clear claim to certainty. The question was, what would it take to convince the USCC, in particular John Verigin, to accept the possibility that Peter Petrovich Verigin (John Verigin's grandfather) may have had a part in promoting and encouraging Sons of Freedom activities?

When Mel Stangeland and Mark Mealing presented a draft statement acknowledging the role that Chistiakov played with the Sons of Freedom, the willingness of the USCC to discuss this statement was the first sign that long-held positions were now negotiable. Agreement on this contentious issue meant that there was a possibility of reaching an accord on the key issue of bombing and burning. How far John Verigin was willing to go to reach an accord was put to the test by the Reformed Doukhobors, who made it conditional that Mr. Verigin would have to sign an undertaking that, in effect, would neutralize the "power of the curse."

Conflict theories, be they in the form of frustration-aggression, social identity, or human needs theory, may have their place in providing an explanation for some aspects of this conflict. For instance, one could argue that frustration might have led to acts of nudity or to someone's setting fire to a building. Similarly, an argument could be made that mass burnings were the result of individuals' choosing to identify with the Sons of Freedom, which, in turn, meant that nudity and the burning of one's home were rites of passage. However, what conflict theories ignore is how individuals come to act in certain ways through certain cultural influences, beliefs, and/or language and symbols.

Resolving the turmoil did not mean isolating issues, as one might in traditional mediation; rather, it meant finding opportunities to merge parts of the competing narratives into a single story. These competing narratives not only acknowledge but also define what being a person in the world of the Doukhobors means.

6

Rendering the Past into Meaning

Meaning is derived through the structuring of experience into stories, and ... the performance of these stories is constitutive of lives and relationships. As the storying of experience is dependent upon language, in accepting this premise we are ... proposing that we ascribe meaning to our experience and constitute our lives and relationship through language.

– M. White and D. Epston, *Narrative Means to Therapeutic Ends*

My objective was to capture the experiential meanings of three key individuals who not only played a significant role throughout the Expanded Kootenay Committee on Intergroup Relations years but who were also instrumental in helping to achieve an accord. I began the interviews (November 2001), at which time I asked them to describe how they came to view the other Doukhobor groups, especially during their earlier years. I was curious to know whether the "storying" of childhood experience would shed any light on their involvement in the EKCIR sessions.

Those interviewed were Fred Makortoff, Jim Popoff, and Steve Lapshinoff. Mr. Makortoff served as spokesperson for the Christian Community and Brotherhood of Reformed Doukhobors (Reformed) and Mr. Popoff spoke for the Union of Spiritual Communities of Christ (Orthodox). Steve Lapshinoff, who was also a member of the Reformed Doukhobors, played an important role in providing a research focus – a role from which all the groups benefited. All three interviews described in varying detail what it was like to grow up in three distinctly different Doukhobor communities within the Kootenay-Boundary region.

Mr. Popoff was raised in Grand Forks among other Orthodox Doukhobor families. Mr. Makortoff grew up in a Sons of Freedom family in

Shoreacres, a small village located between Castlegar and Nelson that consisted of a mixture of Sons of Freedom and Orthodox Doukhobors. And Mr. Lapshinoff was raised in an exclusively Sons of Freedom community called Gilpin, which was located approximately eight kilometres east of Grand Forks.[1]

Reconstructing Childhood

Of the three interviewees, Steve Lapshinoff had the least to say when it came to describing his childhood. I felt at times as though part of him was still in hiding. I am not presuming that he had issues with the authorities, but his quiet demeanor suggested that his experiences may have been somewhat insular compared to those of Fred Makortoff or Jim Popoff. Steve Lapshinoff said that, for the most part, what he remembered about growing up was his fear of fires and stories about the government.

> The government was bad. The government has done this and the government has taken the land away, jailed the people for nothing ... So you are brought up with those things. The police were your enemy. When growing up you had the fear of any stranger that would come in there that you didn't know. You would go away and hide.

An underlying sense of fear permeated the Gilpin community. Sometimes it was generated by authorities, but it was also, as Mr. Lapshinoff pointed out, generated by "your own people, never knowing whether or not you are going to be burned out." When some asserted their will over others in the Gilpin community, it was supposedly for the benefit of all; but still this generated fear. For instance, there was a time when several people came to Mr. Lapshinoff's grandmother to ask whether she would sacrifice herself (meaning burn herself to death) in public as a protest against the authorities.

> So it will elevate the suffering of other people that something tragic happens in the community then the government apparently goes back not as harsh. Those were some of the things. She was told that she being a widow, she didn't have anything. She had two sons but aside from that she had no other ties and if she sacrificed herself it would be to the good of the community.

Growing up in Gilpin was confusing for a Sons of Freedom child, with some family members in one group and isolated from another group, as was the case with Mr. Lapshinoff.[2] He remembered that he was not allowed to visit relatives, even those close by, who were members of the USCC, although he said that his grandfather, who was a devoted USCC member, did manage on occasion to visit Gilpin.

Jim Popoff grew up in Grand Forks, and his childhood recollections were of curiosity and wonderment – a sharp contrast to the fear and rejection recalled by Mr. Lapshinoff. Grand Forks was a community in which at least 50 percent of the population was Doukhobor. Everyone was aware of the Sons of Freedom and always suspected their involvement when a bridge or railway line was destroyed. Jim Popoff remembered that, in 1951, when the railway bridge east of Grand Forks was dynamited, it was once again widely assumed that the Sons of Freedom were responsible. In fact, he recalled that, as it turned out, this was one of the few cases in which the Sons of Freedom were not involved. This explosion not only damaged metal girders but also broke windows for several city blocks, rattling others for at least a kilometre around and waking everyone up. Incidents like this created suspicion within the Sons of Freedom community that the government and/or the non-Doukhobor community were conspiring against them.

Fred Makortoff spent his youthful years living in Shoreacres, where Orthodox Doukhobors lived alongside the Sons of Freedom in a relatively organized and peaceful way. Living next door to each other meant that each year the land needed to be reapportioned in order to ensure that there was enough agricultural land to meet the requirements of the whole community. For instance, if somebody died before spring it was reasoned that the family no longer needed the same amount of land; therefore, its piece would be added on to someone else's whose needs had increased that year.

> It seemed to work fairly well; it would be a heated discussion sometimes and sometimes it would be jokes and laughter – people coming together. By ten or eleven o'clock in the morning they would have it hassled out except for some measurements that they would have to verify and check, and that sort of thing. In the afternoon everybody would go and traipse around while they do their measurements, verify what's happening from the year before.

Although growing up in a Sons of Freedom family in Shoreacres had its challenges, a sense of community seemed to prevail among all members.

Mr. Makortoff's youthful years in Shoreacres were abruptly interrupted in early 1954 when he was apprehended by the RCMP and taken to the

New Denver residential school, where he was forced to live until he was fifteen years old. When he returned to Shoreacres in 1956 he noticed that the community had changed. During Mr. Makortoff's time away John Verigin had decreed that the Orthodox were not to associate with the Sons of Freedom, which many, as Mr. Makortoff recalls, took to heart. The only time this new edict was not followed was during marriages and funerals, upon which occasions differences were set aside.

Politics of Education

During the 1940s and 1950s Sons of Freedom families kept their children at home rather than sending them to school. In September 1953, 147 Sons of Freedom adults were arrested for nudity at a *polatka,* or tent village, several kilometres up the Slocan Valley. One hundred and four children were left behind. These children, as well as a few remaining parents, were transported by bus to an old sanatorium in the small town of New Denver. Many remained there until their parents signed an undertaking that they would send them to school. This stand-off continued for six years.

During this time other Sons of Freedom children who were not attending school were apprehended by the RCMP and taken before the local magistrate who was to determine whether they would be made wards of the state. If they were made wards of the state, then they were taken to New Denver to join the others. Steve Lapshinoff remembers hiding from authorities during this period.

Whenever there was a warning that the police might be coming their way the children in Gilpin would immediately head up the mountain behind their settlement to a cabin that had been built by a fellow named Pete Cazakoff. This cabin was located near the American border, which was a few kilometres from where they were living. Mr. Lapshinoff remembered staying in that cabin for as long as a month and a half when he was about nine or ten. He estimated that about thirty or forty children from Gilpin were affected, and this would have made the logistics of finding a place for them to sleep and food for them to eat rather challenging, to say the least.

As mentioned above, Mr. Makortoff was one of the Sons of Freedom children apprehended by the RCMP in March 1954. He suggested that the five years at the New Denver Dormitory were not as traumatic for him as they had been for some. Before he was apprehended he had learned to read Russian at home as his grandfather had maintained an extensive library. During his stay at New Denver school officials described him as being as bright and articulate with adults as he was with other students. Although he claimed he adjusted well, the downside for Mr. Makortoff was that five years of his life had been taken from him.

Jim Popoff attended public school in Grand Forks and was raised in a family that embraced knowledge and new ideas. His father, Eli Popoff, was a noted historian who wrote about Doukhobor life and culture. His home was a gathering place for scholars and others who came to learn about the Doukhobor people and their confusing politics.

While Mr. Popoff was attending school certain events left a strong impression not only on him but also on the whole community. One such event occurred when Mr. Popoff's childhood friend, Betty Lebedoff, was taken to New Denver by the police: "The police drove right past our place and Betty was sitting in the back with her doll and her head pressed against the window." This left Mr. Popoff and others feeling alienated and confused as they, like most, were unaware of the struggle over the politics of education that was being acted out between the province and the Sons of Freedom at the time.

Sons of Freedom Rite of Passage

Fred Makortoff recalled many visitors to his home, but he remembered one in particular. This visitor dropped by the house on occasion, and Mr. Makortoff referred to him as "old Arishnikoff," a relative who often travelled with Chistiakov to Mexico. "He was an engaging story teller who had been to places and done things that were totally fascinating." His wife (who was Mr. Makortoff's great-aunt) was what he described as a "peculiar lady," a "die hard Sons of Freedom" who would "gather the girls together, especially around [shelling] pea time ... and she would tell them stories" about her experience as a Sons of Freedom. These were "legendary type [stories], some magical moments."

He remembered that, back in the late 1940s, she was one of two women who would go up to the highway or railway tracks and undress, which inevitably caused a commotion. This was her way of protesting – for what purpose, no one was clear. She was finally arrested and spent time in jail. Fred Makortoff remembered that this was considered to have been her initiation rite: "when they would come back, having paid their dues, they now entered the warrior society." As he put it, "if you have hunted your lion you have done your thing" – a rather ironic metaphor for a pacifist culture.

Storytelling provided the cultural fabric that gave the Doukhobor people their identity, linking people to past events and locations. In listening to stories one would learn about "the old battles and how who said what had meaning." A key theme in most stories was Chistiakov and his relationship with the Sons of Freedom. His words had "power" and gave a purpose to those who were looking for their place in the world. Fred Makortoff listened to the many stories about Chistiakov, and only realized later that the stories were not contextualized with regard to events occurring at the time. His curiosity led him to discover more about the past, which proved valuable when the EKCIR sessions were held.

Jim Popoff's childhood friend, Betty Lebedoff, returned from New Denver in 1958 and attended school in Grand Forks with her friends. In 1962 Betty's parents were planning to join the trek to Agassiz, but she did not want to go. The day the trek passed through Grand Forks, Jim Popoff remembered hearing Russian voices singing as the people trekked up the main street of town and passed in front of his school. He estimated that there were somewhere between 800 and 1,000 people participating in the trek that passed through the area.

> I remember that a lot of us ... acknowledged the fact that we felt a powerful draw because the singing was something we could relate to. We even knew some of the people personally. And we could just feel the ambiance, irrational as we knew it was.

Jim explained that the singing was so moving that you could "sense the kind of inner motivational forces that were driving this thing, even though they were not obviously properly balanced or tempered by other processes that should have been in existence."

What Jim Popoff referred to as "inner motivational forces" Fred Makortoff referred to as "fervor":

> I remembered watching people. [Some] got undressed; I never did like that energy. It was one of those ones where it was not focused, it was an erratic energy. It drove people into some kind of frenzy. At any rate I remember that they lit a fire, people throwing things in the fire, people throwing money into the fire to indicate that they weren't into this materialism.

This was a different type of energy than that Jim Popoff experienced. This energy was unbounded, invasive, driven by "politics" as well as by faith.

If one could locate a common energy shared by all Doukhobors it would be their singing: this is what gave the culture its identity and its spirituality. The a cappella voices were both rich and harmonic. The psalm was the voice of the people, which had faded away during the years of turmoil only to resurface during the EKCIR.[3]

In Search of Identity
The ongoing media interest in the Doukhobor situation and the growing concern of their non-Doukhobor neighbours created a demarcation between the Orthodox and the Sons of Freedom that led to intrafamily divisions similar to those previously described by Steve Lapshinoff. As the media generated more and more attention on the burnings and bombings, the USCC implemented a policy of non-fraternization to ensure that people could distinguish between the law-abiding Doukhobors and the "terrorists." For many, the Doukhobor identity was no longer being defined by a belief system, a culture, or tradition but, rather, by media images appearing on the evening news. Jim Popoff recalls that for much of his childhood

> the dominant reality of our Doukhobor identity was the terrorist activity and it permeated our lives in every respect. People even when they didn't legally change the spelling of the last names, informally did so. Kids in school would start spelling their names with v's and ov's just to make it less obvious that they were connected. People would give false names when they would go to work in the Okanagan.

Presumably, changing the endings of their name meant that non-Doukhobors would no longer acknowledge who they were.

Blurring of Identity
Fred Makortoff remembered hearing stories from his grandfather and others about some Orthodox Doukhobors who were also members of the Sons of Freedom.

> [Some of them] had participated in some of the acts, particularly in the forties. There would be stories about who said what and it would be almost legendary type of stories, somebody did this and somebody did that, and somebody just went and sacrificed themselves [sic] for that to achieve this end.

He recalls that, during the 1940s, the common cause for both the Sons of Freedom and the Orthodox Doukhobors was the Second World War. The war effort created a lot of hostility between the Doukhobors, who did not serve in the armed forces because they were granted military exemption, and non-Doukhobors. This hostility occurred mainly during the years of conscription, but it was also apparent when the war ended and the veterans returned from Europe. Many veterans thought that the former Doukhobor lands, which had become Crown lands, should be theirs for the taking, even though Doukhobor families were still occupying them.[4] This led to protests as well as to burnings and bombings that some of the Sons of Freedom believed involved both themselves and Orthodox Doukhobors.[5]

Introducing Stephan Sorokin

In the early 1950s bombings and arson were again on the rise. The RCMP became the new provincial police force in September 1950, replacing the British Columbia Provincial Police. The province was entering into an election and talk about the "Doukhobor problem" was on everybody's agenda. At the same time, the Doukhobor Research Committee chaired by Harry Hawthorn was undertaking its examination of Doukhobor life and a consultative committee on Doukhobor affairs was organized to bring the groups together in order to address immediate concerns.

This all happened at the same time that Stephan Sorokin arrived in the Kootenays amidst much skepticism about his new-found role. The Sons of Freedom accepted him as soon as John Lebedoff introduced him as *Yastrebov*. He was considered by many to be an opportunist and by many others to be the long lost leader of the Doukhobors. As he waded into the melee, everyone watched to see what he would do.

One of the major functions of the Consultative Committee on Doukhobor Affairs was to find a new location for the Sons of Freedom as it was believed that this would bring peace to the Kootenay-Boundary region. The irony was that it was not the Sons of Freedom who found a new home but, rather, Stephan Sorokin who found a new home in Montevideo, Uruguay, where he lived off and on for the next thirty years.

Fred Makortoff recalls the first time he saw Stephan Sorokin. He described him as a man who had a certain charisma, a kind of aura about him, which he thought was unusual: "You could sense that there was something in him that had some sense of mission or purpose. I couldn't quite say what it was. There was a sense of new beginnings and this is where we are going with a new leader and that kind of stuff's happening."

In 1970, when Mr. Makortoff returned to the Kootenays with his wife and children after having lived in Vancouver, he soon encountered Mr. Sorokin. At the time Fred Makortoff was busy building a water system. Mr. Sorokin walked up to him and said, "I need a person, come with me." Mr. Makortoff said, "We got a dam that we need to finish up." Mr. Sorokin said, "No, no, the elders can finish that. We have other things we got to do." Fred Makortoff went on to work for Mr. Sorokin for the next ten to twelve years. This was a time of turmoil between the Sons of Freedom and the Reformed Sons of Freedom who were trying to change. However, it was also a time where there was a sense of new beginnings among the younger families. Stephan Sorokin's mission was "not to allow any of the old thinking and radical types in there," which proved to be a constant struggle.

Jim Popoff had an early experience with Stephan Sorokin when he arrived in Grand Forks in the spring of 1950. Prior to his arrival, Mr. Sorokin had spent a few days in Blaine Lake, Saskatchewan. Jim Popoff remembered that when Mr. Sorokin arrived out west, he had been introduced as a guest from the Ukraine, someone "who spoke a few words and sang a few songs" at the USCC youth festival that spring. Jim Popoff's grandfather, who was chair of the USCC Executive Committee, was often given the task of hosting guests; however, this time he was unable to oblige, so his son-in-law, Eli Popoff (Jim's father), was asked to host Stephan Sorokin. Although Jim Popoff did not remember much about the man or his politics, he did remember "the spats, his white and black shoes, his cane that was partly white, and his shiny beard." He also recalled that it may have been his friend Jim Kolesnikoff's uncle, Anton Kolesnikoff, who later became "a henchman of Sorokin's," who came to the Popoff home and picked Mr. Sorokin up and took him to Gilpin for his first encounter with the Sons of Freedom.[6] From this time, in 1950, Mr. Sorokin established himself among the Sons of Freedom as their "spiritual" leader, but a number of his followers subsequently came to view John Verigin as their "material" leader.

To this day Stephan Sorokin remains a controversial figure. Some believe he helped the Sons of Freedom change their ways, while others believe he was an opportunist who used the Sons of Freedom to serve his own interests.

Influence of the Soviets

Whatever role Stephan Sorokin may have played among the Sons of Freedom, he went to great lengths to convince the Reformed Doukhobors that the Soviet influence among the USCC was something about which they needed to be deeply concerned. Fred Makortoff recalled that

> there was a definite fear, as we could see the USCC moving to a reengagement with mother Russia. And a reengagement, in fact a moving back

there as part of the prophecies that the Doukhobors are one day sup-
pose to do that. Nobody knows when that is going to happen, and is
this the moment? Maybe we should be ready.

One might argue that the relationship between the Soviets and the
Doukhobors made a lot of sense. The Soviets wanted to keep in close
contact with compatriots abroad, and they did so through *Society Rodina*,
as they had done in the 1920s, when they had invited 2,500 Saskatchewan Doukhobor families to return to the Soviet Union to assist with
their collective farming experiment.[7] The Doukhobors, on the other
hand, had kept alive the prophecy that they would eventually return to
the Soviet Union. Thus the relationship between the Doukhobors and
the Soviet Union continued to build.

No one knew exactly what to expect from this closer relationship
between the Doukhobors and the Soviet Union, although the Reformed
were quick to note that a cultural influence was beginning to be felt. It
began with friendship engagements between the USCC and Soviet officials, followed by a barrage of literature. Here, the Reformed noticed
that, rather than simply singing, people began to read musical scores.
This change, Fred Makortoff suggested, was a worthwhile "cultural experience for the USCC folks ... because they learned singing by notes."
These cultural changes were also a concern to some USCC members
because musical accompaniment, such as the use of a piano for Soviet
performances, was now allowed at the USCC community centre in Grand
Forks, and this had been unheard of before.

The one change that riled many people, in particular the Reformed
Doukhobors, was the sudden departure of Peter Legebokoff, the former
editor of *Iskra* (a USCC publication). As Fred Makortoff recalled:

> The thing that broke everybody's back was when John [Verigin] began
> going over there, more and more ... He was a big heavy drinker at the
> time. You could see that [the Soviets] were assuming more and more
> control till he fired Peter Legebokoff. And we realized at that time,
> "Holy smokes this is serious business." They really got him because
> Peter Legebokoff was an innocent individual, [a] very deeply religious
> man and wouldn't hurt a fly kind of guy. But he tried to go through
> *Iskra* to place the futility of and stupidity of both the Soviet and Ameri-
> can positions. They reamed him out. John was the mouth who was told
> to fire the guy and he did, from Moscow. And we went, "Oh, oh, oh not
> good."

The concerns the Reformed Doukhobors had about the Soviet influence on the USCC were widely circulated through their communiqués. Some of the source material from which they drew, especially the Canadian League of Rights, an extremist, anti-Semitic group that operated initially in Ontario and later established itself in Alberta, was spurious and sensational. Jim Popoff did not know Fred Makortoff or Steve Lapshinoff before the EKCIR sessions. Somehow that didn't seem to matter to the Reformed Doukhobors as his name was often mentioned in reference to his role as editor of *Mir* and *Iskra*. The Reformed Doukhobors referred to both publications as "KGB organs" and to Jim Popoff as "a KGB agent under some other disguise, who was under the orders of John Verigin, who was a well-known KGB agent."

Locating the Narrative

After Fred Makortoff relocated his family to the Kootenays in 1970, he took an interest in both national and international politics in his search for answers to some of the questions he was asking himself at the time – questions such as: "Why are we different? Why do we need to be? What was it that was making us special? Or were we just another silly bugger sect defining themselves for some other reason; are we in fact different from anybody? And if so how?"

When he spoke to the elders he noticed that their stories were like events, without a reference point or a link to anything occurring at the time. So he organized what he referred to as a "research party" and went to the *Nelson Daily News* to read everything he could find. His plan was to set out, in historical sequence, the stories that people told, thus creating a framework that he could use for analysis. He went through the *Nelson Daily News* newspapers as well as those of the *Trail Times* looking for reports about the Doukhobors during the Chistiakov era.

During this same period Jim Popoff, along with friends, started a new publication called *Mir*. His interest in his own history sparked him to branch out and to meet some of those who were seen as outsiders and to seek their views. One of the first people he interviewed was Joe Podovinikoff, who was seen by many in the USCC as controversial because his name – more than that of any other save Stephan Sorokin – epitomized everything the USCC disliked about the Sons of Freedom. Joe Podovinikoff had been the "eloquent propaganda spokesman" for the Sons of Freedom and Reformed Doukhobors, whose writings had denigrated the USCC and its leaders. But when Mr. Popoff interviewed him, Mr. Podovinikoff had already cut his ties with the Reformed group and was soon to become a member of the USCC, where he assumed a prominent position. Many, both within the Orthodox and the Reformed Doukhobors, looked upon this with disdain.

Power of the Curse

In 1978 John Verigin was charged with four counts of conspiracy to commit arson. During his trial, many of the Sons of Freedom witnesses who were responsible for bombing or burning community centres, post offices, and other buildings, said that they did so under the threat of a curse. Mr. Verigin and his legal team denounced the "curse" as something that was primitive and superstitious, and generally foreign to Doukhoborism. Mr. Verigin's defence counsel, Harry Rankin, argued that the Sons of Freedom used the "curse" as an excuse to give legitimacy to their actions.

The issue of the curse was raised on numerous occasions throughout the EKCIR sessions. During our interview, Jim Popoff described the "curse" as "an outgrowth of a peasant illiterate culture" – a culture that has its roots in the "superstitions" of centuries past.

> In our USCC Sunday schools ... and it was also discussed in our extended family with my grandparents and great grandparents, we were told that there had been, a century ago, a family that had been particularly active in working against the interests of the leadership during the time of Peter Lordly in Russia. Some of his followers were saying, "Petyushka, look at what these guys are doing to you, and how can that stand?" And he answered that it won't stand, because ... "these people will bring on themselves with this activity seven generations of bad luck, they bring a curse on themselves."

Mr. Popoff explained that the "rationalistic segment of Doukhobor society always viewed the concept of a 'curse' as a more primitive form of saying 'what goes around, comes around.'" In other words, "bringing karma on themselves that they are going to have to deal with for future generations." A common Russian expression, "if you are really upset with a person, [is] 'May you be cursed thrice,' or 'May you be cursed for seven generations,' would be considered a 'serious kind of medicine.'" Mr. Popoff concluded that he "was not aware of any instance of any of the Verigin leaders ... placing a curse on somebody":

> but I know of instances when people who were among their supporters might have said something like, "You're working against Peter

Verigin – You are going to be cursed for seven generations." So, to some people, the association with the leader represented a power to curse somebody.[8]

An acknowledgment of the curse was raised during the final negotiations leading up to the Interim Accord. Fred Makortoff and the Reformed Doukhobors pushed for John Verigin to sign a declaration stating that he "would not curse anybody to commit acts of violence,"[9] which many Sons of Freedom believed he had the power to do. Jim Popoff said that, by 1984, John Verigin knew that people needed to move beyond the old notion of the curse if any form of conciliation was to be achieved. He said he also knew that the only way to achieve this was for him to sign a declaration that he would not curse anybody to commit acts of violence. Hence, the declaratory statement proved to have meaning as the curse was never mentioned again.

Institutionalized Leadership

Jim Popoff suggested that, historically speaking, Russian people in general had difficulty adopting democratic institutions and, therefore, Doukhobor leaders played an important role in providing spiritual guidance to their followers (who exhibited many traditional Russian tendencies):

> The Doukhobor people believed in the Christ spirit living in every human being and later Chistiakov used the metaphor that even when you accept spiritual leaders it's not in the sense that they shine the light and if they go out it is dark. It is in the sense that each of the regular members is maybe a 45 or 100 watt bulb and leaders are 300 watt bulbs but it's all the same energy going through all of them. And so Doukhobors just adjusted to this.

Leadership only became a powerful institution when people believed that leaders had special power. The irony is that the Sons of Freedom, whom Chistiakov described as the most spiritually enlightened Doukhobors, were the most leader-dependent of all the Doukhobor groups. This was evident, in part, when they accepted certain individuals as leaders on the basis of what they thought these people could offer given the stories they would tell – whether these stories were derived from dreams or from the company they kept (usually a reference to the Verigins). The Verigin leadership, as Jim Popoff suggested, was institutionalized by circumstances.

It's like the queen bee concept in a hive. The queen bee starts out like any other bee but they feed her all this stuff that makes a bigger bee out of her – that way she is able to eat five times her weight in food and produce five times her weight in eggs every day. Well, the same thing here. Once you develop an institution then you feed it in terms of supporting it, in terms of giving individuals within that institution certain prerogatives, and a certain kind of prestige and aura.

Following Mr. Popoff's metaphor, the pressure to maintain responsibility in the public eye was so enormous that it took its toll on each of the Verigins, including John J. Verigin.

I think John Verigin ... sometimes may feel bothered that he did a less than perfect job. That he could have done better if he didn't resort to escapism and alcohol at times. A lot of people say that if he didn't have this escapism and alcohol, he might have committed "Hare Kari" thirty years ago because he was dealing with an almost impossible situation. People were expecting things out of him, demanding things from him, imposing things on him, accusing him of things, all of which were contradictory to each other and coming from fifty different directions. John Verigin was in fact instrumental in helping to bring about many of the necessary solutions to existing problems.[10]

Following the EKCIR sessions, John Verigin managed to address his lack of sobriety and has apparently remained sober ever since.

Conclusion

The challenge of growing up as a Doukhobor during the turmoil years was made even more difficult due to the image propagated by media reporting. Jim Popoff knows from his travels and from attending university what it was like to be part of a culture that is spurned by the outside world. Steve Lapshinoff's world may have been smaller than Mr. Popoff's, but it was no less complicated thanks to distorted media images of it. The spurning that he experienced came from relatives, neighbours, and others within the Sons of Freedom as well as from those in other Doukhobor groups. Fred Makortoff's experience was different from those of Mr. Popoff and Mr. Lapshinoff; however, like them he was genuinely curious about his own identity and what it meant to be a Doukhobor. He exercised his curiosity by exploring beyond the boundaries of his own experience to assemble the stories he had heard into a pattern that included the past.

A quality that was evident in all three interviewees was the desire to learn. Unlike many in their respective groups, who lived in insular worlds built on the stories that they told each other, these three men were never satisfied. This leads to the question of whether there were other qualities evident in some of the Doukhobors that might help these groups address their conflicts.

Jim Popoff noted that he respected certain people who, during the EKCIR sessions, had helped him to understand the nature of the problems being discussed. He mentioned Olga Hoodicoff and Polly Chernoff as examples of those who had had their own epiphanies during the process and who had had the courage to recant some of their earlier beliefs. Fred Makortoff and Steve Lapshinoff challenged his assumptions and perceptions, not maliciously but respectfully, and also were willing to make concessions of their own. Others, like John Ostricoff, "was also able to ... call a spade a spade, and talk heart to heart when it was required." These are qualities that are not discussed in the conflict literature; yet without them the likelihood of reaching an accord is very remote. This became evident once Fred Makortoff and Jim Popoff left the sessions.

7
Turning Points of Reason

Epiphany: a sudden and important manifestation or realization.

– Oxford Canadian Dictionary

The objective of this chapter is to identify the epiphanies, or turning points, experienced by Fred Makortoff, Jim Popoff, and Steve Lapshinoff during the Expanded Kootenay Committee on Intergroup Relations sessions.[1] Denzin (1989) suggests that an epiphany may occur as a result either of a major event or of cumulative experience. Both types of epiphanies could be observed at the EKCIR sessions.

Throughout the interviews I noted certain things that Mr. Makortoff, Mr. Popoff, and Mr. Lapshinoff held in common. For example, all agreed that the EKCIR was designed to encourage the discussion of stories and to enable people to challenge assumptions. They all recognized the importance of meanings, especially when it came to constructing a new understanding of Peter Petrovich's role among the Sons of Freedom. Fred Makortoff and Jim Popoff were both affected by the death of Mary Astoforoff and both ended their involvement at the EKCIR sessions.

The interviews provided me with new insights into the challenges that each Doukhobor group faced at different times throughout the EKCIR sessions. I learned that the challenges for Fred Makortoff and the Reformed Doukhobors came at the beginning of the sessions, when they were trying to decide whether or not to participate. For the Reformed, the uncertainty involved whether the process would be manipulated by the government or whether John Verigin would "get his way" with the non-Doukhobor representatives. In the end, Mr. Makortoff concluded that the process had not been unduly influenced by any of the groups.

For Jim Popoff, the struggle of the Union of Spiritual Communities of Christ (Orthodox) came towards the end of the sessions, when it was deciding how badly it wanted the accord. The challenge for John Verigin was to explain to his members, who had spent many years guarding their communal properties, the need for this accord.

Structure of Engagement

Jim Popoff, Fred Makortoff, and Steve Lapshinoff all agreed that the EKCIR played an important role in bringing about a change in the patterns of communication between the Sons of Freedom, the Reformed, and the Orthodox communities – a change that made it possible to bring an end to the bombings and burnings. The EKCIR structure allowed each of the Doukhobor groups an opportunity to tell about its experiences with burnings and bombings in a mutually constructed and agreed upon manner.

Fred Makortoff believed that the structure of the expanded KCIR suited the Doukhobors' need for a consensual approach to conflict resolution, which, he added, fit the cultural makeup of the Russian *Mir*. He thought that the structure was "official enough" to remind everybody that this was not simply a "meeting of the commons."

> I immediately sensed that this is something that could work. It had the psychologists there, the police were there, [and] the mayors were there. It had all the elements brought together to succeed. So then it depended on where we go from here.

Mr. Makortoff explained that the initial expectations and attitudes that many had of the EKCIR were drawn from their experiences with Judge Sullivan's 1947 royal commission, which he described as being "very hierarchical."

> This is what people were used to and had no reason to expect anything different. You came and it was done to you and you left. They did what the hell they wanted anyway. If it comes out good, hey fine. If not, well we knew that anyway.

Both Fred Makortoff and Steve Lapshinoff thought that the EKCIR created what was termed a "neutral place" rather than a "huge wall," which Fred Makortoff euphemistically described as "something [one] threw rocks over trying to hit somebody on the other side." "Now you could bring all of the stuff to the 'table,'" he said, "which provides a quality of difference when you are fighting an enemy that's got eyes ... We are in a mess. Let's define what this mess is. What are the components of it and see if we can find solutions to it." This pretty well indicates how apprehensive everybody felt when the sessions began.

All the sessions were recorded and the transcripts of the proceedings were distributed at the end of each session. This, according to Mr. Makortoff, gave the sessions a sense of importance and helped to inform those who had not attended:

> One of the things I enjoyed was that there was a record of who said what; all of a sudden when you say something it somehow counts. We come from an oral culture and to our people it made a huge difference because we are no longer trading our own stories. Our own stories have now become black and white. They are no longer oral stories; they are no longer malleable either. You see what I mean. In an oral culture, in an oral tradition, an oral way of being the way we were, you could create the same experience, you could create different kinds of meanings.

Mr. Makortoff described the "table" that people sat around as a placeholder for the past. "The moment of truth," he suggested, "occurred when stories were told that were only known among certain people." What was significant was that "the words spoken could not hide as they were now part of a transcript of what people said."

Although the record became a repository of individual narratives, at first most people didn't understand much of what was occurring. Fred Makortoff said that many initially saw the sessions as semi-legalistic, which left numerous people confused. It took two or three sessions before they began to sense that what was occurring was different from what they had expected.

The conundrum for Doukhobor people, given their dismal historical relationship with governments (both in Canada and in Russia), was that they were being asked to tell their stories with the provincial government's being present. As Mr. Makortoff recalls, participating in a forum with the government created a "sense of betrayal, particularly because some of the stuff that was going to be discussed involved leadership and leadership roles."

> You're going to say that your leader's an asshole, what the hell does that make you? This is your brightest and your best? That takes a lot of courage. And to break with a tradition of closed-mouthed-ness where

you don't divulge these secrets with your family, with your friends or even with them at the USCC, particularly with them at the USCC, then why do you need to tell this to government. What good does that bring to either the USCC or us?

In other words, it took a great deal of courage for people to come forward and relate their experiences. One example Mr. Makortoff highlighted involved Polly Chernoff's presentation. Not only was her story eloquent but it also took "enormous guts" for her to say the things she did, when she described how she was forced to continue with burnings to ensure the safety of her family, even though she was jeopardizing her health in the process.

When that kind of revelation occurred the whole session took on an earnestness and seriousness that ... helped define, yes this is serious business folks. We are going for it. It's going to happen. That brought a lot of the other people out of the woodwork that were going to sit back and watch ... Hmmm. Maybe it is time to say. A lot of people came forth.

Challenging Assumptions
Fred Makortoff was cognizant of conducting a balancing act in representing the Reformed group as he had to be cognizant of both those who wanted revenge and those who recognized that the EKCIR sessions needed to serve a higher purpose.

I convinced most of them that we need to be seen not as the Gauls attacking Rome, so to speak ... [I]f you are going to do it you got to do it in a logical fashion and you got to particularly come from a whole different side, if you are coming from a side of vengeance it's not going to work and if it's a principled action then [we] cannot lose. But if it's a non-principled action, if it was becoming one of hate, I will get that son of a bitch, because I spent time in jail, or that vengeance kind of thing, you are going to be seen for what it is, that is a cheap trick and none of this is going to work.

Mr. Makortoff said that many people remembered the prophecy about "a big round table where a lot of stuff was going to come out ... a day of reckoning, if you will, of this whole Doukhobor problem." This gave the sessions a sense of status that, to this point, they had not had. He went on: "Things are going to get paid attention to and things need to be said and ... words are going to count." However, in order for the process to truly work, people needed to feel that there was a higher-level plan – one that did not favour any one group. As Mr. Makortoff recalled, it had to be "a big round table where everybody could see everybody and there was enough firepower around the table in terms of personalities and responsibilities," which he indicated meant that people were to be held accountable for their words.

Fred Makortoff assumed that when he told his side of the story people there would instantly recognize the problem and would know how to resolve it. Of course, the situation wasn't as straightforward as he had thought. One of his first epiphanies occurred during the initial session when he realized that telling his side of the story was not enough to convince his listeners. For instance, he recalled Mr. Nevokshonoff's story about Peter the Lordly's involvement in the burning of schools. "I was challenged about that immediately by John [Verigin who] said no such thing, you haven't proven anything. It's all hearsay. At that point I realized, 'Oh, oh, this is going to be long, drag out type of an affair.'" As Mr. Makortoff learned, this exercise was not so much about storytelling as it was about learning how to position one's story. Positioning one's story meant recognizing that it was part of a sequence of stories and that it had its place in raising the consciousness of the listener.

Negotiating Meaning

For Jim Popoff, proof that the process was working came when the first EKCIR agreement was reached regarding Chistiakov's role among the Sons of Freedom during the 1930s. Although John Verigin denied there was ever a relationship between the Sons of Freedom and Chistiakov, confusion arose when the KCIR presented some of Chistiakov's "unofficial" speeches.[2] These were the speeches that, prior to his death, Chistiakov told those who were with him that he wanted removed from the files.

Although these speeches had certain meanings for everyone, the Sons of Freedom assumed that parts of them were meant only for those whom Chistiakov had described as "more highly evolved." These were the people he referred as the "Sons of Freedom" and who, according to him, "cannot be slaves of corruption." Statements such as these reinforced the notion among the Sons of Freedom that they had a prescribed role in helping to save Doukhoborism. For John Verigin to agree that there could be different interpretations of Chistiakov's speeches represented a significant departure from the position he had been maintaining all along.

Jim Popoff admitted that he was surprised at the willingness of John Verigin to acquiesce on such an important and extremely contentious issue – one that had separated the Sons of Freedom from the mainstream Doukhobors for years.

> I remember we were all surprised that John Verigin "signed" a statement that included the idea that not only did [Chistiakov] make statements that could have been misinterpreted, but one of the points ... is that he [Chistiakov] should have been aware that they could have been misinterpreted, and therefore ... held partly responsible for allowing statements that could have [been] misinterpreted to go out to the people. And I thought Jeez, John Verigin's willing to sign it! That is really much further bending backwards than we ever expected him to do. And as a result of that, you know, by that point things were beginning to go more smoothly down the highway.

In Pursuit of an Interim Accord

Jim Popoff, Fred Makortoff, and Steve Lapshinoff all agreed that the key epiphanic event at the ECKIR sessions was the signing of the Interim Accord. Jim Popoff described the challenges the USCC went through both internally and at the sessions.

> At that time when [John Verigin] presented [the notion of an accord to the USCC] in the early eighties, we had just gone through the trial.[3] We hadn't finished paying off the debts connected with some of the burnings and bombings and the trials and all the rest of it. The people are saying "What?" "We haven't even paid off all the debt; we still owe $275,000 for rebuilding the centre."

John Verigin argued with his members that they had to do this. "It's better for us in the long run. It's better for everybody, because if we hold these recriminations we are only going to perpetuate the very situation." He knew that he needed to address the ongoing tension once and for all. As Jim Popoff explained it:

> The USCC members were always accused by the Sons of Freedom of being holier than thou; of being the self-righteous ones, saying we're the good guys and you guys are the bad guys. And certainly I grew up with that feeling that there were good Doukhobors and bad Doukhobors and the good Doukhobors were the USCC. Well I later became aware that some of the Sons of Freedom were brought up the same way in

thinking that they are really the only good Doukhobors because they are the only ones willing to put their heads on the line, and believing that USCC members had sold half of Doukhoborism down the river and they just think they're the good Doukhobors.

Jim Popoff described Mr. Verigin as being very clear with his members regarding the intentions of an accord, arguing that they needed to find a beginning point and a common purpose with the Sons of Freedom and Reformed Doukhobors. As Mr. Popoff explained, Mr. Verigin's approach to the other groups was to insist that

> we are not talking about who is holier than thou. In your own way you thought you were suffering for the cause. We don't agree with your way. But we grant you that you've got the right to be wrong in your own way ... We come together on a common point that we want to have Doukhoborism that doesn't involve any bombs, any burnings, any of this stuff and let's start clean from this point. So he presented this memorandum of reconciliation somewhere in '83 as I recall.

Many questioned John Verigin's sincerity with regard to ending the arson and bombings. The Reformed Doukhobors, in particular, believed that the only way to test his resolve was to see whether he was willing to sign a declaration stating that he would not curse anyone. After a long discussion with his members John Verigin agreed to do this. According to Mr. Popoff,

> J.J. had to actually sign a statement to say that he is not going to curse anybody, which he was willing to do despite the fact that he had never cursed anybody before, or wasn't planning on cursing anyone after, and didn't believe in that curse – as I don't believe in it, and most ... other Doukhobors don't believe in it. But he did that because he was aware that some people do believe in powers of curses and still do today in the twenty-first century, never mind in the twentieth.

Testing the Interim Accord
Jim Popoff had an epiphany when he learned that the Interim Accord was being taken seriously by the Reformed Doukhobors. The USCC received a call at its office one day (back in either 1984 or 1985) from the Reformed, who informed them of two Sons of Freedom women who were out on parole and who managed to slip away from those "supervising" them. The USCC had already had watchmen on all of its

properties but thought that the women might also target Fruitova School, which had recently been renovated. Previous threats to the school had been made, but there were not enough volunteer watchmen to go around.

Two watchmen were immediately posted at the school to guard the building throughout the night. Soon after they left the school the next morning, two women appeared and set fire to both their clothes and the building. These fires were extinguished by a neighbour who had witnessed the commotion. Although there was some damage to the building, Jim Popoff was pleased that the Reformed Doukhobors had warned him in advance, and this raised his hopes for the accord.[4]

Mary Astoforoff's Death

Approximately a year after the accord was signed in 1984, Mary Astoforoff, Tina Jmaiff, and Mary Braun went on a hunger fast at a federal prison in Matsqui, British Columbia. Ms. Astoforoff developed complications during the fast and was rushed to a nearby hospital, where she died a short time later. I managed to contact Fred Makortoff and Jim Popoff by telephone to discuss whether all three Doukhobor groups should make a joint effort to talk the other two women out of continuing with their fast. The thought at the time was that, given their deteriorating health, they too might not last that long. Jim Popoff remembered later in the day receiving a call from Fred Makortoff, who, along with several other members of the Reformed Doukhobors, was on his way to Vancouver. He asked Jim Popoff if he was going to join them so that they could make a more fully representative effort to talk the women into ending their fast, which took Mr. Popoff by surprise:

> I said, "I can't just go off like that, you know." And they said we have room for one person and you are the person and you should come along and it will be an opportunity for us to prove in practice that we can work together and so on and so forth. So I phoned J.J. ... He says, "If you are willing to do it, I think you should do it." But he says, "You are not going as an official representative of the USCC because we don't have time to get their approval, we probably wouldn't get the approval from the people." And he says, "If it is successful we will praise you. If it's not successful and there is some kind of catastrophe, then you are on your own."

Mr. Popoff decided to go, so they travelled to the coast together, staying in the same room and eating in the same restaurants. They succeeded in talking the two women out of their fast and returned home as friends.

Manifesting Change

After the accord was signed everyone agreed that the next key issue involved explaining the death of Peter the Lordly Verigin – an event that had resulted in years of retaliatory destruction. The EKCIR Joint Research Committee was established, comprising representatives from each of the Doukhobor groups and the KCIR. The role of this committee was to search through archival sources for information that would shed light on the death of Peter Verigin and to try to come up with possible theories as to why this incident may have occurred. My role was to assist the committee in gaining access to materials that had been restricted for the past sixty years. As Fred Makortoff recalls, this was a new beginning because it no longer pitted one group against the other but, rather, was mutual and exploratory: "It was a stroke of genius creating that [research] committee that was neutral in a sense and [whose purpose was] to dig at stuff together. That gave us some thinking and talking time [with each other]."

To assist the new research committee in its work two workshops were arranged at UBC. One was a communications workshop while the other was a research techniques workshop. The communications workshop proved to be important as it gave the representatives of the Doukhobor groups an opportunity to learn about perception and meaning, which offered them new ways to engage with one another. All of these efforts continued to foster new relationships between the representatives.

Relations between the Doukhobor representatives continued to build over the many weeks and months as they read through archival materials.[5] The down side of this was that their efforts separated them from their own communities, which were not prepared to accept change so readily. For instance, as the representatives continued to work together, their own constituencies became concerned as various stories began to circulate. Some accused their representatives of being used by the other groups, while others quietly applauded the possibility of change.

Dénouement

Both Fred Makortoff and Jim Popoff left the EKCIR in 1986. The turning point for Mr. Makortoff came soon after Mr. Sorokin's death, when he met with the Reformed Doukhobors to discuss the role he was expected to play at the EKCIR sessions. He explained to them that his loyalty had been to Mr. Sorokin, who had been supportive of the direction that he was taking. However, he went on to explain to them that he would have trouble speaking on their behalf as he might not agree with what they were asking him to do. Some understood what he meant while others remained baffled, wondering if he was asking for money. At this point he realized that he had to make a decision as to whether or not to continue.

> I said, "Look folks. I can't go where you want to go with this stuff. I cannot in my heart of hearts support some of the ideas that are here. They are yours. They are very dear to you, you need to speak to them, you need to illustrate them, and you need to make the necessary arguments for that position. I can't and I won't do that for you because I don't believe that way."

Once he made his decision to resign, rather than telling his community first, he decided to make his announcement at a research committee meeting where representatives from all the groups as well as the government were present. As Mr. Makortoff indicated, it was at this point that he became persona non grata within his group.

The next time that Fred Makortoff and Jim Popoff were together was at an event held at the USCC community centre in Brilliant, following an EKCIR session. As Jim Popoff recalls, during breaks John Verigin would slip into the bar, which was across the hall from where the session was being held. On the last day of the session Mr. Verigin invited everyone to a luncheon at the USCC Cultural Centre in Brilliant. This was the first time the Reformed and Sons of Freedom had been invited to a USCC function. Some of the Sons of Freedom attended but the Reformed declined the invitation. Fred Makortoff, however, who was no longer representing the Reformed Doukhobors, was willing to make the gesture. But when the time arrived to go to the centre Mr. Makortoff became less and less comfortable. When he saw Jim Popoff, Robin Bourne, Mark Mealing, and me conversing about the day's session, he approached us to note his concern:

> "Look here's the situation. John is in his cups. He's torqued right out. And he's going to stand up, and it's his home turf, his ball park and he will go out there and rant and rave in front of his own folks and he is going to say silly, stupid things. I am not going to be able to let him, if I'm just sitting there, and then who the hell am I. I'm going to stand up and counter, saying, "What the hell do you think you are doing?" And it's an embarrassing thing to do that to a person who has invited you over for a meal at his place. So I would rather not engage in this whole bullshit. Why would I be going and embarrass him in front of his folks and create an ass out of myself.

Jim Popoff, who understood Mr. Makortoff's position, said:

> I will make you a deal that if he starts saying something untoward,
> something off line there, we won't embarrass him or anything but you
> have a right to stand up and walk away and I will stand up and come
> with you. And by us both walking away I think there would be a fairly
> loud statement made around – you are out of line again and you are
> losing it. A lot of folks would see that without having to rant and rave
> back and create an argument.

As it turned out, surviving the meal without fanfare or embarrassment was the least of Mr. Makortoff's worries that day and for a long
time after.

> When we got back here to the Settlement (where we lived at that time),
> whoa there was a hullabaloo. I betrayed the community. I was a turn-
> coat. I went into John Verigin's pocket; all of that kind of stuff ... They
> were afraid of me because I was a sharp tool that could be used for or
> against them. So they began the discrediting process as quick as possi-
> ble because they didn't know what was happening there as I was sitting
> next to Jim at their cultural centre, when I wasn't even at the KCIR
> meeting. They were immediately afraid and their first reaction was to
> immediately discredit them – an interesting strategy. It is useful in groups
> like that and people use it all the time.

He decided he had had enough of the "back-stabbing" that was rampant among the Reformed Doukhobors. A short time later, he and his
family moved out of the New Settlement.

Jim Popoff's departure from the EKCIR by the end of 1986 was not as
eventful as was Mr. Makortoff's. Mr. Popoff explained that he had assumed additional responsibilities as editor of *Iskra* and as executive assistant at the USCC office. In view of all this, he had difficulty spending
sufficient time with his young family, which he hoped he would be able
to do if he dropped some of his commitments, such as the EKCIR.[6]

The coincidence was that both Jim Popoff and Fred Makortoff left at
about the same time. I presumed that the Orthodox and Reform communities could not reconcile the notion that progress had been made
and that relationships were beginning to form among those from different groups.

As the EKCIR continued to meet during this period, other events occurred. There were numerous pleas on behalf of family members and

the Sons of Freedom community to help those who had been imprisoned for arson. Many believed that if the women were allowed to participate in the sessions they might support the efforts that were being made to end the burnings and bombings. All three Doukhobor groups made a joint request to the corrections authorities to release the women into the care of their families, with the support of the communities. In each case, when the women were released, whether to Gilpin or to Krestova, the community assumed responsibility for their care and safety, which in the end proved valuable as it brought the groups together for a common purpose. Overall, the women's participation in the sessions did not shed further light on the matters under discussion; rather, they were intent on continuing with the fires even though they were no longer able to convince others to join them.

The last session was held in September 1987. At the end of it I advised Robin Bourne that the EKCIR had made about as much progress as could be expected. Without Fred Makortoff and Jim Popoff, the sessions were not nearly as constructive as they had been. Overall, I believed that there had been too many changes for the communities to absorb all at once and that time was needed for people to reflect on what had happened.

Conclusion

The turning points helped to provide context and to add new insights into some of the events that took place during the EKCIR years. The sessions seemed to work best when the groups were directly involved in designing and planning them. They enabled the groups to challenge the expectations each had of the other and, thus, were able to take people to the point where a collective statement about the role of Peter Petrovich Verigin was possible. From here, a new relationship among the groups emerged, first, when a collective decision was made to respond to the death of Mary Astoforoff and, later, when opportunities were created that allowed the groups to work together toward a similar goal.

The ECKIR sessions came to an end when it became clear to the province that there was no further progress to be made. This was not a joint decision on the part of the Doukhobor groups involved but, rather, was made by the chair after Fred Makortoff and Jim Popoff left, which was when it became evident that relations between the groups were starting to deteriorate. The assumption was that the groups needed time to accept the changes that had occurred.

8
Conflict and Terrorism: Lessons for the Practitioner

In analyzing the competing narratives that surfaced during the Expanded Kootenay Committee on Intergroup Relations as well as the meanings that emerged in the interviews with key participants, two essential themes emerge. The first concerns the narrative construction of identity among the Doukhobors and how it was derived, with particular emphasis upon the notion of the "terrorist." The second concerns narrative meaning and conflict and how, on further examination, there is a need to challenge our assumptions about how we think about conflict and the interventions we choose when faced with a conflict setting.

Theme 1: Narrative Construction of Identity
White and Epston (1990) suggest that we cannot have direct knowledge of the world; rather, what we know is gained through experience, which we construct in the form of stories. It is through the "storying" process that the teller ascribes meaning to experience. The challenge for those who are in search of facts occurs when the story is more a distortion of the storyteller than a depiction of his or her experience. Hence, discerning "truth" from "fiction" can be problematic, as is discussed by Maude (1904), Shulman (1952) and Franz (1958). Answering the question "what is truth" often leads to philosophical meandering; however, the question cannot be avoided. The notion of truth has "power" and with power comes uncertainty. So, as I waded through the stories that were told I realized that I needed a litmus test to determine whether or not a story could be confirmed.

In my study, a story's confirmation was based on how well it stood up to scrutiny, especially during the EKCIR sessions. For instance, Lucy Maloff denied that her husband had a relationship with the Sons of Freedom or that her son had ever spent time in jail. Similarly, Harry

Voykin denied sending messages to the Sons of Freedom and yet invited them to his restaurant. In both cases, confirmability was addressed when the groups challenged the inconsistencies in Ms. Maloff's and Mr. Voykin's accounts.

Disassembling the Notion of Terrorist

There has been much debate surrounding the word "terrorist" over the last few decades, mainly over the selective context in which it has been used. For instance, the Orthodox Doukhobors were always quick to note that the Sons of Freedom were terrorists and should be treated as such, meaning that the provincial government should take responsibility for bringing terrorism to an end. The nub of the debate occurs when the term "terrorist" becomes interchangeable with the term "freedom fighter." Using the term "terrorist" as a focal point, I draw on Juergensmeyer's (2000) use of the terms "worldviews," "cultural context," and "community of support." My aim is to "disassemble" the socially constructed notion of "terrorist" by examining the Orthodox Doukhobor and Sons of Freedom worldviews and how the Sons of Freedom, in particular, came to adopt certain beliefs. I am interested in examining the circumstances that influenced the nature and direction of the community and how those outside the Sons of Freedom group may have offered (or not) some form of recognition or moral justification to the group's endeavours.[1]

My contention is that individual acts of terrorism, especially those that are culturally or religiously based, do not occur in isolation. These acts, as Juergensmeyer (2000, 11) suggests, require an "enormous amount of moral presumption for the perpetrators ... to justify the destruction of property." My assumption is that the Sons of Freedom did not perceive themselves as acting in a frivolous manner; that is, within their group there existed both conviction and social acknowledgment. The question that the EKCIR wrestled with was this: is it possible that these destructive acts were, intentionally or not, receiving approval from a legitimizing authority; and, if so, what purpose did this serve?

Worldviews

Over 400 years of history helped form the worldviews held by Doukhobors living in Canada, who have certain distinguishing qualities that separate them from other groups.[2] First and foremost, the Doukhobors are Russian-speaking, and they are vegetarian, pacifist, have a communal lifestyle, and believe that the spirit of God resides within each individual. Some of their distinguishing principles, more pronounced upon their arrival than they are today, are their refusal to swear an oath of allegiance, to own land individually, to register births and deaths, or to participate in military-like exercises (whether these exercises were held in a community or in a school). Along with these principles is the significance of certain symbols of faith common to all Doukhobors, the most notable being bread, water, and salt, which represent the basic staff of life – a "toil and peaceful life."[3]

There are other symbols, most particularly the symbol of fire, that have become known over the years, especially among the Sons of Freedom. Cathy Frieson (2002) suggests that burning was a common practice among Russian peasants, who often used it for purposes of justice or revenge, or to exert social control over those who would violate village norms. Then there are the covert symbols used to connote fire and bombings. Some of these symbols include the colour "red," whether worn as clothing, used in a logo on a letterhead, or used in an expression (such as "erecting a pillar of fire from the ground up to heaven," which Mr. Hremakin reported hearing). Some symbols and/or cultural practices have evolved over time and may not be practised to the same extent as they once were. Nonetheless, all of them are defining features of the social identity of both the Orthodox Doukhobors and the Sons of Freedom Doukhobors.

Identifying the Sons of Freedom as "terrorist" was meant to distinguish those Doukhobors who were involved in fire and bombings from those who were law-abiding, presumably the Orthodox and non-aligned Doukhobors. Fred Makortoff told the EKCIR that not all Sons of Freedom were involved in these activities (even though all were at some point branded as terrorists) and that some spent time in prison for crimes they never committed. Furthermore, distinguishing the Sons of Freedom from the Orthodox Doukhobors was difficult as the former, unlike the latter, had no membership list.

The USCC frequently used the term "terrorist" to describe the Sons of Freedom, and at times it was used in conjunction with other descriptors, such as "insane" or "hardened criminals."[4] The backdrop to these views is the USCC's long history of denouncing bombings and arson and their numerous efforts to differentiate themselves from this radical group. The blurring of identities became problematic for the USCC and other Doukhobors when the media described the Sons of Freedom activities as the "Doukhobor problem" and when images of arson, bombings, and nudity were transmitted worldwide. To counter these media images the USCC made innumerable efforts to distance themselves from the "terrorists" and pressured the government to take action against them.

The outsider's view of the Sons of Freedom provides additional support to the view of the Orthodox Doukhobors. For instance, Dr. Shulman (1952) describes the Sons of Freedom as (1) individuals who are aggressively bent, who have failed to satisfy their needs, either as USCC members or as Independents; (2) individuals who are passive, lonely, or guilty and who have submerged themselves in a formless mass of Sons of Freedom in order to atone for their wrongdoings; (3) individuals who are pathological and who would not be tolerated in any society; (4) individuals who are aged, who lack special training, and who have no self-esteem; and (5) individuals who are emotionally impoverished and constricted. In other words, the Sons of Freedom do not conform and are, essentially, social outcasts.

For his part, Dr. William Plenderleith describes the Sons of Freedom as outcasts who were ostracized by their parent body (the USCC). He believes that this outcast state shaped their attitude towards society: "To compensate for this feeling of personal inferiority, they set themselves on a plane that made them feel superior,"[5] which led them to become martyrs to a cause. As he noted, "soon they discovered that the best way to achieve public recognition was to employ anti-social, attention-getting devices, such as dynamiting, arson and nude parading." And he concludes that these anti-social practices enabled "the fanatical Freedomite ... to exalt himself to a stage where he could assume a cloak of superiority and moral righteousness."[6] These "expert" views, along with others, helped to shape public policy for years to come.

The Sons of Freedom believed in the Doukhobor principles, in particular those espoused by Peter "the Lordly" Verigin. They believed that these principles were common to all Doukhobors and that it was their mission to help maintain them in order to save "Doukhoborism." Obviously, this meant countering those who were undermining these principles.

Most of the USCC had a different view of the situation from that of the Sons of Freedom. They believed that the Sons of Freedom were a radical fringe that had very little to do with the Doukhobor faith. Some believed that the Sons of Freedom were influenced by deviants and criminals who had somehow found their way into their midst. The Reformed Doukhobors, on the other hand, accused "the USCC members [because they were] denying the fact that these principles were mutual principles" and that the Sons of Freedom "were the front army people that went out and defended these principles."[7] They also viewed the Orthodox leadership as being responsible for influencing the Sons of Freedom to commit destructive acts.

Over the years, there were many influential Doukhobors, including many among the Sons of Freedom, but none was as important as those involved in the Verigin leadership. We know that Peter "the Lordly" Verigin occasionally referred to the Sons of Freedom, but the group was relatively small during his time. This was not the case when Chistiakov arrived in Canada in 1927, when the number of Sons of Freedom had grown significantly (Tarasoff 1963). Chistiakov appears to have viewed the Doukhobors not as arsonists or nudists but, rather, as the vanguard of the Doukhobor faith. Consider the speech he delivered in the village of Brilliant on 27 January 1929:

> The Freedomites are the head with the horns, the farmers the tail and the Community people the belly filled with filth. The Freedomites are thirty-five years old; such the master can trust. He can put them onto a binder, place the reins in their hands and they can work. But Community Doukhobors are fifteen years old and the farmers only three. The master cannot entrust a binder to such people because they have not grown up. They may let go of the reins, wreck the binder and kill themselves. The Freedomites are worthy.[8]

Although this speech was one of a number of speeches that John Verigin said were purged from the collection at Chistiakov's request, it raises the question as to why Chistiakov would choose to do this. Was this an attempt at redemption or was he being influenced by his grandson, John J. Verigin, who recognized the confusion to which this could lead? But if John Verigin was attempting to mitigate confusion, then why did the USCC continue to publish in *Iskra* slogans such as "Sons of Freedom shall not be slaves of corruption"? Such slogans were seen by the Sons of Freedom, not unreasonably, as a signal that their role in protecting Doukhobor principles was still being publicly acknowledged, if not publicly affirmed.

According to the numerous witnesses who were heard from during the EKCIR sessions, Chistiakov's speeches and the symbolism with which they were imbued had existential meaning for the Sons of Freedom, which conceivably explains why they viewed themselves as different from other Doukhobors. By referring to them as the "ringing bells" (presumably an allusion to their religious zeal and idealism), Chistiakov sets them apart, implying that they are more spiritually evolved than are other Doukhobors. Notwithstanding this special status, Chistiakov and other Verigin leaders publicly rebuked the Sons of Freedom for their "irrational acts" of violence. This public chastisement demonstrated the leaders' interest in perpetuating a particular view about the Sons of Freedom. Whatever the truth might be regarding Chistiakov's role, it had somehow become lost amidst the blurred images of Doukhobor history.

Cultural Context

The cultural context of the Doukhobor community determined its nature and influenced its direction. Without question, the most invasive influence on the Doukhobors involved government policy and enforcement. Governments were perceived as secular bodies whose mission was to destroy Doukhoborism through enforced schooling, removal of lands (in the early 1900s in Saskatchewan and in the late 1930s in British Columbia), and the 1924 CPR train explosion. In each of these examples, the government was seen as the responsible agent, and, in the case of the 1924 CPR train explosion, the government and the CPR were held to account through decades of bombings.

The cultural context of the Doukhobor community was defined by a disjuncture between what the Orthodox and Sons of Freedom Doukhobors were told by the leadership. For instance, the Sons of Freedom maintain that they were told not to buy land, even though the Orthodox could do so. They were told that they would have "the blood of Lordly Verigin" on their hands if they sent their children to school, yet the Orthodox sent *their* children to school. The Sons of Freedom were chastised in public, yet in private they were encouraged to "continue their efforts to remove the dark clouds over them" and to "erect a pillar of fire from the ground up to heaven."[9]

The cultural context was influenced by the introduction of radio and, later, television. Television created strange and frightening images of fire and nudity, and this made it difficult for those growing up Doukhobor to maintain their Doukhobor identity.[10] Jim Popoff, for example, was tormented by the repeated images of nudity, fire, and destruction, and this was exacerbated by the ethnocentric views of the public and the constant mockery of his friends and peers. The Doukhobors were no longer defined by their beliefs but, rather, by media narratives, which led to John Verigin's imposing a "non-fraternization policy" among his members to ensure a clear distinction between those who were terrorists and those who were not.

The Sons of Freedom were physically removed from the Orthodox community, yet, as mentioned above, distinguishing between those who were Sons of Freedom and those who were not was often challenging because not all of the former practised nudism or committed acts of arson or bombings. Consider what happened in the 1940s and 1950s, when many Doukhobors believed that the jails were a means of fulfilling the Doukhobor prophesy of returning to the motherland. Hundreds of Sons of Freedom were imprisoned during this period, many for crimes they did not commit. For example, Fred Makortoff told of two Sons of Freedom men sitting together on a bench. One fellow had spent five years in prison for a crime he did not commit because the other fellow had had him convicted in order "to save him so that he could go [back] to ... mother Russia."[11]

Part of the cultural context at the time involved Sons of Freedom intimidating other Sons of Freedom, like Polly Chernoff, for example, who spoke about her home being set ablaze with her grandchildren trapped inside. She reasoned that the fire was set because she had refused to continue burning, even though she had stopped due to ill health. Other examples involve Steve Lapshinoff's grandmother, who was asked to sacrifice herself in order to get the government's attention, and Mike Bayoff, who shot a guard in the hand when he and others were out to destroy Peter the Lordly's tomb in March 1944.

What kept the Sons of Freedom involved in burning and bombing is difficult to say. Fred Makortoff believes that someone in a leadership role had to be privately encouraging them to continue. The reason why they continued committing and suffering for these acts had to do with their expectation that some day everything would be explained. As Fred Makortoff pointed out, "Doukhobor people have for many decades been talking about a promised time and a 'round table' ... when all their loyalties and trust in their leadership and all their suffering would be accounted for."[12]

For the USCC to continue its dominant narrative, certain meanings needed to be sustained among its members and among the public-at-large. If the USCC wished to elicit support from non-Doukhobors or from the government, then the division between the Orthodox and the Sons of Freedom Doukhobors had to be seen as unequivocal. This meant that, as reasoning with other Doukhobors had proven to be futile, the Sons of Freedom had to find other ways to "get their message out" concerning how they were being treated not only by the government but also by the USCC leadership. The media and the trials became their venues. However, the non-Doukhobor public did not appear interested as it had already developed an unsympathetic view of the Sons of Freedom thanks to the many years of destruction and turmoil.

Up until the late 1960s the Sons of Freedom directed their anger towards the provincial government. From 1964 to 1970, while key Sons of Freedom members were in jail, all was quiet. This continued until soon after the release of the men from Agassiz Mountain Prison in the early 1970s, when, with many looking for answers to their imprisonment, Sons of Freedom turned their anger towards John Verigin. This did not necessarily occur because Mr. Verigin had any answers, although many assumed that he did, but because ten to twelve years of prison life had taken its toll on the health and families of the Sons of Freedom, and many believed that the Orthodox leadership was in some way responsible for this.

By 1983, after three years of EKCIR sessions and continuous USCC denials of their involvement, the Sons of Freedom affirmed that they were not interested in being seen, as Peter Astoforoff remarked, as "Mr. Black" while other groups were seen as "Mr. Clean." If the Orthodox Doukhobors wanted a declaration of reconciliation, then they would have to acknowledge their role in Sons of Freedom actions. The Sons of Freedom were determined to have the conflict recognized as one of mutual responsibility. This meant that, if there was to be an end to the violence, then change needed to be co-managed by all of the groups involved, including the provincial government.

Community of Support

A question often asked is: was there a link between the Orthodox Doukhobor community and the Sons of Freedom that the latter could reasonably have interpreted as support? There were many stories that suggested that Doukhobors who were not Sons of Freedom supported Sons of Freedom actions. Nick Nevokshonoff, for example, explained that it would have been very difficult, if not impossible, for the Sons of Freedom to have destroyed all the schools in one night back in 1923 without the support of other Doukhobors. The Sons of Freedom, he argued, were too few and had no means of travelling to where each of the schools was located.

More openly, Peter "the Lordly" Verigin acknowledged the Sons of Freedom as a threat in a letter that Samuel Verishagin sent to the minister of education in May 1923. Although Mr. Verishagin's signature was on the letter, it was widely known among community members that the letter had been dictated by Peter Verigin. It stated: "we cannot guarantee that the schools will not be burned." For the Sons of Freedom and Reformed Doukhobors, this meant that Peter Verigin had endorsed the actions of the former. John Verigin, on the other hand, argued that Peter Verigin was not endorsing their actions but, rather, simply indicating that, because the Sons of Freedom were beyond his control, he could not guarantee that something would not happen. Whatever view one might hold, the Sons of Freedom served a political purpose at the time, even if that was only to caution the provincial government about its aggressive educational policies.

Another example of community support of the Sons of Freedom is Peter N. Maloff's relationship with Chistiakov and his liaison with the Sons of Freedom. His 1950s writings provided insight into his involvement with the Sons of Freedom and his reasons for ending it. His writings also provided insight in the 1980s, when the USCC decided to bring Lucy Maloff to the EKCIR sessions to clear her husband's name. Her public denial of his involvement with the Sons of Freedom led many to wonder what she thought this would accomplish and why she thought "the people" would believe what she had to say.

During the early 1980s, there was the liaison between USCC executive members and Sons of Freedom members. Remember Harry Voykin, who on occasion invited the Sons of Freedom to his restaurant. The story was that Harry Voykin asked Sam Shlakoff to bring Mr. Hremakin, but when the latter arrived at the restaurant Mr. Voykin ignored him. The Sons of Freedom reasoned that Mr. Voykin's asking for "Hremakin" did not mean that he was interested in the old man but, rather, that he was interested in finding dynamite as, in Russian, "Hremakin" derives from the word *hremet* (phonetic), which means "to make noise."

Then there was John Verigin himself, who admitted having had contact with key Sons of Freedom members who were responsible for destroying USCC property and other buildings. For instance, he admitted that he corresponded with and visited those who were living in the tent village at Agassiz Mountain Prison. Years later, he talked to Olga Hoodicoff, who went to his home to find out whether or not the instructions she had received from John Savinkoff were correct. On other occasions he met with Peter Astoforoff. Mr. Astoforoff claimed that, on two of these occasions, Mr. Verigin had instructed him to destroy certain buildings. Although Mr. Verigin acknowledged that he had met with those mentioned, he "swore" that he had never instructed or counseled them to burn or bomb. In fact, he pointed out that these same stories had been discounted as evidence at his trial.

With regard to former leaders, Mr. Verigin was adamant that there was no evidence to link Chistiakov to Sons of Freedom allegations. One can only presume that he believed that there was no documentation to support their claim. And one may also presume that he knew that he had the support of the general public, the Doukhobor people generally, and federal and provincial politicians, who later conferred on him the Order of Canada and the Order of British Columbia. But knowing this, why did he change his mind and agree that Chistiakov may have played a significant part in helping to shape Sons of Freedom attitudes?

There may have been a number of reasons why John Verigin changed his mind. First, the witnesses that the USCC presented provided more questions than answers. As mentioned above, Lucy Maloff appeared to be revisionist when she did not accept what others already knew and when she refused to acknowledge what her husband had written, even though it was part of a collection of his writings that he had donated to UBC.

Second, Mr. Verigin's use of alcohol was becoming more and more problematic. Peter Astoforoff said that he only received instructions to destroy certain buildings when he and Mr. Verigin had been drinking. And, at the 10 September 1984 KCIR Planning Committee meeting, Mr. Verigin's conduct raised questions among the KCIR and others in attendance concerning why he chose to interact as he did with certain Sons of Freedom members. One of these members was Mary Astoforoff, who had set fire to the Doukhobor Museum in Ootischenia, and the other was Peter Savinkoff, who was an indicted co-conspirator at Mr. Verigin's trial. These activities had been noted by the non-Doukhobor people who were present at the time, and they began raising questions about the disparity between Mr. Verigin's actions and words.

Third, Mr. Verigin had not realized that there was documentation on file at UBC – in particular the speeches of Chistiakov, which Mr. Verigin thought had been purged from the collection but that, in fact, had been donated to the university. There were also reports in the provincial and federal archives pertaining to the correspondence of the Doukhobor community's lawyer, Peter Makaroff, QC, and numerous RCMP documents that tied Chistiakov to the Sons of Freedom.

Mr. Verigin could have maintained that, in all cases, the evidence was circumstantial. However, if his purpose was to end the conflict, then his interactions with certain Sons of Freedom members, both prior to and during the ECKIR sessions, led some to wonder aloud what his intentions really were. We know that whatever was said between Mr. Verigin and the Sons of Freedom resulted in the latter's claiming one thing and the former another. So why did he continue to engage with them? One possible reason is that John Verigin and the Sons of Freedom depended on each other to justify certain ends. The Sons of Freedom needed direction, purpose, and moral support in order to function, and Mr. Verigin needed to stop his members from assimilating with the mainstream non-Doukhobor community. This is precisely the type of situation in which, Simmel (1955) would suggest, reciprocal antagonisms are important in maintaining unity. Was Mr. Verigin using his apparent victimization to try to keep the membership of his community from declining further (e.g., via intermarriage)?

The relationship between the Sons of Freedom and the USCC was as much familial as it was political, and my contention is that neither party knew how to extricate itself from this long history of cultural entanglement. Mr. Verigin had become burdened by his reliance on alcohol and the Sons of Freedom were looking for any sign that affirmed the notion that there was a connection between them and the USCC. Perhaps, in the midst of all this turmoil, Mr. Verigin was in search of a *deus ex machina* – a role that the KCIR would eventually assume.[13] Or was the KCIR the little dog Toto, from the *Wizard of Oz*, who pulled away the curtain to reveal the true wizard. Whatever the case, in the end, by acknowledging the possibility that Chistiakov had encouraged the Sons of Freedom to be "the vanguard, the ringing bells, the guys that made noises far, far away,"[14] Mr. Verigin began to remove a cultural burden from himself and his members as well as from the Sons of Freedom.

Theme 2: Narrative Meaning and Conflict

As we move from narratives about the Doukhobors to conflict generally, the aim is to "deconstruct" the notion of conflict and narrative discourse. Conflict theorists have often defined conflict as "opposing interests," "goal divergence," and "unmet needs." Needs emanate from a psychological discourse, whereas interests and goals are reflective of a discourse on political economy, all of which has been decontextualized to serve a rational, linear thinking, and problem-solving framework for conflict resolution. The question that for me remains unanswered concerns how conflict emerges from human interests and needs (Burton 1990; Fisher and Ury 1981) or, for that matter, from unattainable goals (Tjosvold 1991; Folger, Poole, and Stutman 1996; Pruitt, Rubin, and Kim 1994)?[15]

Conflict by Any Other Name

I propose that competing interests, needs, and goals are a mere synthesis of experience between two or more individuals and do not necessarily have much to do with the conflictual patterns or competing narratives. I am not suggesting that competing interests and unmet goals do not lead, in some instances, to conflict; rather, I am only pointing out that these self-interests are essentially *differences* constructed from meanings at which individuals have arrived based on certain assumptions they have made. For conflict to emerge there must be other factors that compel one to act in a conflictual way.

These other factors might begin, for instance, with some cognitive predisposition, bias, or perception. However, for differences to manifest themselves in conflict there has to be an intentional act or an emotional reaction to what has been said or done. This is not to suggest that an intentional act is not without emotion, only that in the case of the Sons of Freedom Doukhobors, their actions were seen as a calculated defiance, regardless of how they were feeling at the time. Burnings and bombings were *intentional* acts that emanated from meanings and assumptions that someone (or a group) had constructed, based on some set of circumstances. These circumstances could consist of oblique messages, confirming or disconfirming information, dreams that someone had, a growing fervor about saving Doukhoborism or "returning to the Motherland through the jails." Here, language is a political act consisting of signs, symbols, and metaphors, all of which distinguish Sons of Freedom discourse from the discourses of others.

Within the Space of Meaning

To understand how we arrive at "conflict" we need to explore how the notion of "self," in being with "others," comes to experience conflict. If we presume that conflict emerges when someone acts on her/his assumptions, and that assumptions are based on meanings created from perceptions, biases, or other circumstances, then the question is: where do *meanings* come from? Lakoff and Johnson (1999) tell us that meanings emanate from a cognitive-embodied process and that they are expressed though metaphors.

If meaning is cognitive-embodied, does this presume that it is also culturally embodied? Again, Lakoff and Johnson (1999) tell us that metaphors are used to provide clarity and cultural context with regard to abstract ideas. Here, the creation of meaning is interconnected, both internally and externally, to other factors. Internal factors might begin with a genetic predisposition but include perception, sense-making, and other meaning-creating processes that are influenced by beliefs, values, and other mediating influences[16] that have been adopted and refined over time. In other words, the cognitive-embodied process is influenced by an individual's culturally embedded sense of identity, and both are situational to one's environment. Environment, in this case, refers to structural conditions such as sensory feel of space and time; compliance (or non-compliance) with social norms and cultural expectations, rules, and regulations; as well as relational patterns evoking discordant narrative themes.

If our purpose is to understand how we come to experience conflict with others, then we need to understand the interrelationship between self and others, which is influenced by cultural traditions and belief systems as well as social structures and hegemonic practices. I believe that we cannot separate the individual from her environment as the individual *is* her/his environment. In the same sense, you cannot separate the individual from the influence of cultural elements, from her/his own cognitive processes, or from the interactions she/he has with others.

In order for change to occur one has to recognize the linkage between four factors: namely, identity, cultural influences, relational patterns, and the structural conditions that make up one's epistemology. Where I diverge from my colleagues in the conflict field is in my belief that, if we are to address the complex conflict settings within which we find ourselves, then there is little purpose in decontextualizing the stories we tell ourselves and others and turning them into abstract units called "issues"; rather, we need to look for new ways to engage with others beyond the superficial and the subliminal.

Conceptual Framework

Fiske and Taylor (1991) have found that, when people encounter an ambiguous situation, a certain framework of beliefs, emotions, and experiences influences how they create meaning. For instance, when the EKCIR was examining the events that led up to the 1924 CPR train explosion that killed Peter the Lordly Verigin, I found myself confronted by the Sons of Freedom argument that the Canadian government had assassinated Lordly. Although this was one of a number of theories presented during the EKCIR sessions, no matter what disconfirming evidence was provided, the Sons of Freedom were not to be convinced. Why? First, they had already reasoned, given the government's previous history with them, that the government and the CPR were the likely saboteurs. Second, since no charges had been laid and since access to these files had for many years been restricted, it was believed that this case was part of a government cover-up. Story constructions such as these become mythic representations – a conceptual framework that shapes perceptions and meanings. These same representations helped the Sons of Freedom justify bombings of government or CPR-owned properties over a fifty-year period.

Narrative Discourse

If we were to examine narrative discourse we would see that it has its own structure – one that is culturally derived, intertextualized,[17] and situated within a specific historical and conceptual framework. We would note that narrative discourse has rules and conventions that differentiate it from opinions, statements, descriptions, lyrics, and recipes. We would also note that the manner in which stories are told varies from group to group and from region to region. Hence, when we examine narrative discourse among the Doukhobor groups, we find that it contains common elements that reflect certain beliefs, cultural practices, and metaphors; however, we also find that it contains differences regarding how each group uses symbols, signs, and codes that represent ways of functioning specific to how each group defines itself in relation to others. Whether there are similarities or differences, narratives often remain the same in their telling until they are reconstituted, after new insights have been brought to bear. For example, when I returned to the Kootenays after many years I revisited some of its historical sites, one in particular being Peter Verigin's tomb, which had been dynamited in the 1930s and 1940s. More than twenty years ago, when I visited the same site, the story told by the caretaker had it that the Sons of Freedom were responsible for the explosion and the victimization of the Doukhobors overall. This time, when I returned, there was no mention of the Sons of Freedom having played a part in this event; rather, the caretaker talked about individuals who took it upon themselves to create havoc for unknown reasons. Even when I probed for more detail, I noticed that he was very gracious in his narrative treatment of the Sons of Freedom as a group. His rendering no longer included the term "terrorist," or any of the other negative descriptors often used, which suggests to me that stories constitute an ever-changing field that serves to define how we see ourselves and others.

For the conflict resolution field, this means recognizing that reducing narrative to issues to be "resolved" might work well for some disputants and the "intervening party" if the problem to be addressed is well defined. However, when a complex set of circumstances prevails, the conflict resolution process itself hinders conversation by narrowing rather than enabling stories and their meanings to unfold. This was evident at the EKCIR sessions, where we listened to witnesses tell their stories. For many it was about getting to the truth by challenging the facts and circumstances; however, for the people telling the stories, it was more about removing a burden that they had carried for some time, thus enabling them, if only for a moment, to ask themselves and others what it was all for.

The Metaphor
Fiske and Taylor (1991) and McNamee and Gergen (1992) posit that an individual constructs her/his conceptual framework through language. With regard to language, Lakoff and Johnson (1999) tell us that metaphors, being grounded in human experiences of time, space, and physical objects, are the means of providing a sense of clarity to an abstract idea or concept. David Leary (1984) describes metaphor as the "giving of one thing or experience to something else, on the grounds of some proposed similarity between the two."[18] So, for example, when a "conspiracy" metaphor is used, it consists of language drawn from an array of experiences and beliefs common to both the individual and her/his surrounding group or culture. Thus, the "conspiracy" metaphor patterns one's perceptions as well as organizes how one conceives the situation that he or she encounters. Phrases such as "bringing them to their knees" and "out-manoeuvring them," or metaphors of "war" or "competition," embodies language that shapes the social identity of the self in relation to one's "storying" experiences of the other.

Shulman (1952), who applied a "diagnostic" or "disease" metaphor to the Sons of Freedom, best illustrates the impact of metaphorical concepts. He concluded that the Sons of Freedom were suffering from "autism[, which] radically interfered with a realistic appraisal of any situation ... allow[ing] them to substitute naïve wishful thinking" (144). As autism was considered to be "incurable," this meant that nothing further could be done with adult Doukhobors; therefore, the only possible solution was to "cure" the children by exposing them to mainstream culture through education – an initiative undertaken by the BC government a short time after Shulman's report was released.

Creating a Meaning-Based Approach to Conflict
How does the Doukhobor experience inform our understanding of conflict?

1. The importance of analysis in understanding the dimensions of conflict
There are many possible ways to view a conflict situation, each of which invites a different approach to intervention. The question is: What does one need to know before deciding to intervene? Although the conflict literature is replete with conflict resolution models, it offers little in the way of analyzing complex conflict situations.

There have been some attempts to create a conceptual framework for conflict analysis; however, most frameworks are used as guidelines in which "parties," "issues," and their "interests" are identified. These are frameworks that focus on the entities involved in the conflict but not necessarily on the relational space between them, where meanings and judgments are created. These are frameworks that do not acknowledge such external influences as culture, beliefs, symbols, and codes, which shape how we perceive and process meaning. They do not acknowledge such external influences as structural conditions – be they rules, conventions, policies, or other factors that influence how we conceive and act within our environment. And they do not acknowledge how we engage with others in relational patterns and how each factor influences other factors within an integrative whole rather than as separate parts.

	Self	Other
Internal	Identity	Relational patterns
External	Cultural influences	Structural conditions

Each of these influencing factors is inseparable from the other, meaning that they represent the epistemology of who we are in our interactions with others. This implies that the "self" is shaped and formed in relation to whom we think of as the "other."

Analysis must consider the nature of the conflict setting, whose story is featured and whose is not, as well as what pretext and subtext are foundational to the conflicting narratives. The focus should *not* be the entities – that is, the parties – but, rather, the relational space between them. These include the dilemmas and paradoxes that emerge, which may have little to do with individual choice but that become conditions that must be understood in order to adequately address the conflict setting.

For instance, there were stories circulating among the Doukhobor groups about returning to the motherland through going to jail. Many Sons of Freedom members began admitting to crimes they didn't commit or implicated those who hadn't been involved in order to ensure that they would be included in the return to the motherland. We must consider what gives life to these stories and what purposes they serve. Without a broad context it is very difficult to know what intervention strategies one should consider without falling victim to one's own biases and presuppositions. Hence, an analysis should provide a basis upon which to decide whether or not an intervention is required, and if so, what direction it should take. Are the conflictual elements relational patterns that have emerged from perception and meaning; or from cultural influences, biases, and beliefs; or from structural conditions that may need to be altered? An analysis may be all that is needed for participants to gain insight into the nature of their competing narratives.

2. Designing a structure for presenting conflicting narratives
What is clear is that there were no advantages to imposing a structure on the Doukhobors. Such structures had been imposed before without "success." How a structure is designed is especially important when there is a perceived power imbalance among the conflicting groups. Involving the participants in the design process may enhance support and increase the likelihood of the participants' assuming responsibility for its progress.

The question is, what considerations should be given to the design of the space that is to accommodate the participants during the intervention process? What meaning does space create among the participants? Should there be others (e.g., observers) besides the key participants? What rules might there be for those observing? Should the sessions be recorded, transcribed, and made available to those not present? The notion of transparency is often not addressed to the degree that it should be, especially where a lack of trust is endemic. In such situations transparency is paramount.

If the conflicting narratives have historical relevance, or if there is a need to circulate stories to others, then creating a transcript or public record is an important consideration. If assurance is needed that the stories are truthful (rather than imagined), then an oath, or affirmation, or some other culturally sanctioned means of verification should be considered. When a story or testimony is presented within a structured setting there may be a need for continued dialogue (or even negotiations) outside these sessions.

3. Determining the role of the intervener
The intervener role ideally functions through the "authority" conferred by the participants. In conferring such authority, the implied expectation is that participants are willing to suspend their disbelief in order to allow the process to unfold. This means that the participants' and the intervener's roles are well understood and agreed upon at the outset.

This also means that the intervener assumes responsibility for ensuring that the process is consistent throughout. If conditions allow, the intervener acts as both a participant-observer and a participant-facilitator, which means that judgments are suspended and a priori assumptions/ solutions are not imposed.[19]

4. Asking analytical questions about the conflict narratives

Asking analytical questions assists the participants in reflecting on various aspects of their stories and the meanings they create. The key role for the intervener involves assisting participants to become conscious of the discourses that are foundational to their views and to see how discourse and cultural influences shape the conflict narratives that they relate. This may be done by viewing the conflict narratives as meaning-based, exploring the underlying assumptions out of which meanings are created, and thus allowing the parties to "expand the conversation" towards possibilities that may not have been previously aired. This is quite different from viewing narratives only with respect to their truth claims.

5. Changing the metaphorical concepts

The use of concepts such as "terrorist" or "conspirator," or the use of metaphoric language that connotes war or competition, influences certain perceptions that, in turn, impede understanding or change. Substituting such usage with metaphors like "journey" or "path," or metaphors that connote working or travelling together, helps participants to align their perceptions and this, in turn, increases the likelihood of co-managing the conflict and achieving a mutually agreeable outcome.

6. Producing change in language and perception

Changing the metaphor is the first step towards helping participants change their perceptions of themselves and others. The next step is to identify opportunities for altering the well-established patterns of interaction, such as encouraging participants to work on issues together. In the Doukhobor situation, getting the groups involved in joint learning sessions and joint research sessions enabled new patterns of communication to emerge.

7. Conflict is not for "resolving," but for recognizing, differences

Focusing on narrative meaning helps us to understand differences in perception and how these differences came about. Understanding is enhanced when participants recognize the subtext of their views and how it has been culturally maintained.

8. Conflict viewed strategically and creatively
Co-creating a structure of engagement creates consonance among participants. However, there may be times when an impasse emerges. At this point, perturbing the process can create strategic advantages that assist the parties in moving from their entrenched positions. One example of this took place during an EKCIR session when the chair raised his concern over the lack of progress. What this did was to impose a time frame, which functioned as pressure to make a decision. This shifted the responsibility for the process from the chair to the groups themselves. By creating dissonance he was able to force the issue, which led the participants to hold a discussion to determine whether or not they still had something in common that they hoped to achieve.

9. Certain human qualities may be needed for reaching an agreement
There are certain human qualities that are important if an intervention is to achieve a mutually acceptable agreement. These include being curious rather than judgmental, acting in a trustworthy and respectful manner, and acting as if all of the participants are equals. For instance, Jim Popoff said that there were certain people who had helped him to understand how they came to view the situation as they did. By way of example, he mentioned Olga Hoodicoff and Polly Chernoff, who, in reaching their own epiphanies, trusted the process enough to tell their stories, even though this put them at risk. He noted that Fred Makortoff and Steve Lapshinoff challenged his own assumptions and perceptions not maliciously but respectfully. He also noted that the non-Doukhobor members, in particular the KCIR, acted on their curiosity by querying the groups to explain how they came to hold certain views. These are human qualities that are not discussed in the conflict literature, yet without some demonstration of them, the likelihood of reaching an accord would have been lessened considerably.

10. Achieving agreement through reimaging
An effective intervention process is one that "break[s] up our sense of certainty that we know all that can be known about what we mean, or even more dangerously, that we know what someone else means" (Winslade and Monk 2000, 141). A successful intervention culminates in some form of agreement, which is nothing more than an abstract, symbolic statement that offers a mutual point of intersection. This

intersection is where the participants engage in a reimaging of group identity. This helps the participants "let go" of their misconceptions and misunderstandings, allowing for the emergence of new relational patterns. The challenge is in the implementation, where the focus is on actions rather than on words to produce change.

Conclusion

What is apparent is that, for the past eighty years, certain stories were told that were used to explain one group's relationship with the world ("real" Doukhobors) while dismissing that of others (terrorists). The crux of the debate was the Sons of Freedom claim that their mission was to save Doukhoborism and that they were acting on behalf of the leadership. The Orthodox Doukhobors, on the other hand, insisted that "these people" were "mentally deranged" and that their actions had nothing to do with being Doukhobor. When the competing narratives were aired at the EKCIR sessions the distinction between identities became less clear, but the need to clarify and to affirm them became paramount as more stories emerged. Through negotiating the use of language a historical nuance was changed, which, for the Sons of Freedom, meant that the burden they had carried had been lifted enough to allow for the possibility of moving in the direction of an accord.

Once an accord had been reached, constructing a new relationship among the participants was a gradual process that began with the groups' agreeing to work together on common issues, the first being the 1924 CPR train explosion. However, notwithstanding good intentions, the process of change is difficult to gauge if one has to stand still to observe. Steve Lapshinoff (and his partner Ann Sorokin) said that it has taken at least a decade for change to be noticeable. They noted that social events were now being held, bringing the Sons of Freedom, Reformed, and Orthodox Doukhobors together (seventeen years after the accord was signed). John Verigin, who gave up drinking shortly after the EKCIR sessions ended, retired from the day-to-day operations of running the USCC, leaving the work to his son John Verigin Jr., who wished to see the groups unite. Through young John Verigin's efforts, and the efforts of many from each of the groups, changes in the pattern of relationships between the groups were becoming evident.

A recent example of unification occurred about a year prior to my interviews (2001), when the Krestova Men's Choir, a blend of Reformed, Sons of Freedom, and former members of these groups, decided to sing together on the understanding that "no politics or [personal] agendas" could be discussed. This was in itself unusual as the Krestova community consisted of ill-defined and dissenting subgroups. The men's choir first performed at a Mother's Day event in Krestova, where several USCC members were in attendance. This event generated talk in both the Krestova and Orthodox communities, the topic being that it would be nice to someday sing together. Excitement was evident but no one was certain how to make this happen until Fred Makortoff, from the Krestova Men's Choir, and Lawrence Popoff, from the Kootenay Men's Choir (USCC), who had known each other for years, chatted and then spoke to their respective groups about the possibility of staging an event in which they would try to sing a couple of songs together.

To begin, the Krestova Men's Choir invited the Kootenay Men's Choir (along with their spouses or partners) for an evening together at the Krestova Hall. Fred Makortoff emceed the event, which he described as magical, with humour, singing, and baked pies being the recipe for change. Then the Kootenay Men's Choir reciprocated a short time later, inviting the Krestova choir to its hall in Brilliant. This was the first time a Sons of Freedom or Reformed group had, on invitation, entered a USCC hall. "It was a moving event," Fred Makortoff recalled, adding that John Verigin Jr. helped foster this new beginning.

All three of the men I interviewed spoke enthusiastically about the event and the subsequent efforts to reinforce this new beginning. Fred Makortoff said that a sense of unification was starting to permeate discussions in their communities; he described a "feeling that has finality; [one] that addresses and speaks to a large inner part of the individual. It is what people have hungered for, for a long time."

They also spoke enthusiastically about the new "Tri-Choir," which consists of members from all three groups, and that was organized soon after their festival performance. The men get together every week, in each other's halls, on the understanding that politics will not be discussed. Fred Makortoff describes the experience as "almost euphoric." "The split that used to happen out of Krestova isn't there anymore," although he admits that "the old war horses still emerge once in a while but they are talked down."

Jim Popoff recalled that when it was decided that the three choirs would attempt their first joint rehearsal, the groups agreed that it should be held at the USCC cultural centre in Brilliant.

> The members of the Brilliant Cultural Centre, some of whom had kicked those same men out of that yard a mere ten to twelve years ago, met them on the front steps and there was a hundred percent shaking of hands with every person before they walked in ... This was an emotional

scene. All mature men were there, but there was a few teary eyed looks
... because they felt the impact of the moment.

He added that "this was a turning point, a milestone in Doukhobor
history."

Although there is considerable work left to be done to achieve reconciliation with the provincial government and to help repair the psychological trauma suffered by those who spent time in the New Denver
dormitory, work towards repairing fractured relationships among family members within the various Doukhobor communities is clearly under way. Whatever we imagine conflict to be, one thing is clear: it is not
about "resolution" but, rather, about recognizing differences that must
be co-managed by those involved. Timing is an important element because one needs to know that the desire for change is stronger than the
desire to perpetuate a "culture of conflict or violence." I was recently
asked whether the intervention worked because the timing was right. I
thought about this for a moment and then replied that the notion of
time is but one of many integral factors that presents itself on various
occasions. But time alone is not a recipe for change. As Fred Makortoff
suggested, people had hungered for this gathering for a long time. And
yet it wasn't time, the accord, or dialogue that created change. These
phenomena represented opportunities to alter conditions, to construct
new stories, and to enable the emergence of new relational patterns,
especially for those participating in the process. However, change, as it
is now being observed, did not occur until Doukhobor people were willing to trust themselves enough to embrace their own life force as
Doukhobor people. And it was the harmonic merging of their voices in
song that set this change in motion. As I ponder this further, perhaps
"choir" is the appropriate metaphor for addressing conflict and change.
A choir is both a place and a gathering of people. It has a structure, a
history, and tradition as well as shared cultural influences. Yet, it is also
subsumed by narratives, has its own discourse, and requires discipline
and practice if harmony is to be achieved. For the Doukhobors, choir
represents a past that has finally found its beginnings.

For me, conflict involves stripping away the cultural veneer of unex-
posed assumptions, dropping the notion that there are specific models
and best practices that should be used, and removing the rigid prescrip-
tions and techniques of conflict resolution practices. It also means being able to assume more conflict and uncertainty and to reflectively
engage one's own epistemology. The world needs more meaningfulness, not less, to help us move on.

A Survey of Bombings and Burnings: Doukhobor and Sons of Freedom Communities, 1940-83

Date	Incident

1940

May 23 Cooperative Growers Exchange in Robson, BC, destroyed by fire

Oct 5 Store in Shoreacres destroyed by fire

1942

Nov 11 Grain elevator in Brilliant destroyed by fire

Dec 9 Sawmill at China Creek destroyed by fire

1943

Apr 15 Krestova school damaged by fire

Sep 5 Bomb found in Slocan Park School

Dec 12 Jam factory in Brilliant destroyed by fire

Dec 13 General store in Brilliant damaged by fire

Dec 13 Doukhobor meeting house and packing shed damaged by fire

Dec 13 Gas station in Brilliant damaged by fire

Dec 13 Garage in Brilliant damaged by fire

Dec 13 Six CPR boxcars in Brilliant damaged by fire

Dec 26 Packing shed near Castlegar destroyed by fire

1944

Jan 31 Attempt made to burn J.J. Verigin's residence in Brilliant

Feb 6 CPR train station at Appledale destroyed by fire

Feb 6 Gilpin school damaged by fire

Feb 6 Krestova no. 5 village damaged by fire

Feb 10 Krestova school damaged by fire

Mar 3 Verigin's tomb – guard shot in hand

Jun 3	Verigin's tomb damaged by explosion
Jun 7	Second attempt to dynamite Verigin's tomb
Jul 29	Verigin's tomb destroyed by an explosion. Two guards assaulted

1945

Jun 7	Four Krestova dwellings destroyed by fire
Jun 7	Krestova no. 2 village destroyed by fire
Jun 7	Krestova no. 4 village destroyed by fire
Jun 7	Goose Creek dwelling destroyed by fire – woman died of burns
Jun 17	Highway bridge over Slocan River damaged by explosion
Aug 3	Pass Creek water system damaged by explosion
Sep 2	Mike Bayoff dwelling destroyed by fire

1946

Apr 21	Doukhobor community hall near Grand Forks damaged by fire
May 12	Doukhobor hall in Grand Forks destroyed by fire
May 12	Doukhobor hall in Thrums destroyed by fire
May 12	Doukhobor hall in Passmore destroyed by fire
May 12	Garage and store in Perry Siding destroyed by fire
May 12	Doukhobor hall in Perry Siding destroyed by fire
May 12	Doukhobor hall in Claybrick destroyed by fire
May 14	Goose Creek store and bathhouse destroyed by fire
May 15	USCC dwelling destroyed by fire
May 17	Doukhobor community hall in Glade destroyed by fire
Jun 11	Doukhobor community hall in Shoreacres destroyed by fire
Jun 12	Brilliant water pipeline bombed
Jun 29	Doukhobor community hall in Brilliant set fire by 150 Sons of Freedom
Jun 30	Krestova no. 2 village destroyed by fire
Jun 30	Krestova no. 4 village destroyed by fire
Jun 30	Krestova no. 5 village destroyed by fire
Jun 30	Three Krestova dwellings destroyed by fire
Jun 30	Mike Bayoff dwelling burned by owner
Jun 30	Krestova sawmill and five houses destroyed by occupants
Jul 21	Sons of Freedom hall in Gilpin destroyed by fire
Jul 21	Five homes in Gilpin destroyed by fire
Aug 1	Shoreacres dwelling destroyed by fire
Aug 8	Peter Maloff's storage shed and barn damaged by fire

1947

Mar 13	Grand Forks Golf Club damaged by fire
Apr 16	Grand Forks log storage shed damaged by fire
May 11	Grand Forks Russian school and seed storage shed damaged by fire
Jul 21	Verigin's tomb damaged by explosion
Jul 25	Water pipeline in Brilliant damaged by two explosions
Jul 29	Shed burned in Slocan Park and Koch Siding
Jul 30	Doukhobor community hall in Glade destroyed by fire
Jul 31	Glade school damaged by explosion
Aug 6	John Lebedoff dwelling destroyed by fire by 100 Sons of Freedom
Aug 7	Mike Bayoff dwelling burned by owner
Aug 8	Passmore dwelling burned by owner
Aug 10	Krestova no. 3 village destroyed by fire
Aug 10	Sproule Creek school and teacherage destroyed by fire
Aug 10	Krestova dwelling destroyed by fire
Aug 12	School at Erie destroyed by fire
Aug 12	Goose Creek chicken coop destroyed by fire by 100 Sons of Freedom
Aug 12	Multiple dwellings destroyed by fire
Aug 13	Krestova dwelling destroyed by fire
Aug 13	Farmers Exchange building destroyed by fire
Aug 13	Krestova no. 1 village destroyed by fire by 100 Sons of Freedom
Aug 14	Krestova grain elevator destroyed by fire
Aug 15	Winlaw school – attempted arson
Aug 15	Two Goose Creek dwellings burned by owners
Aug 16	Two Krestova dwellings burned by owners
Aug 17	Shoreacres hay barn burned by owner
Aug 17	Shoreacres blacksmith shop burned by owner
Aug 17	Flour mill in Krestova destroyed by fire by thirty Sons of Freedom
Aug 18	Shoreacres chicken coop burned by owner
Aug 19	Shoreacres dwelling burned by 150 Sons of Freedom
Aug 20	Blewett chicken coop destroyed by fire
Aug 22	Two Shoreacres dwellings burned by sixty Sons of Freedom
Aug 23	Shoreacres no. 3 village destroyed by fire
Sep 7	Gilpin barn burned by owner
Sep 8	Five barns in Krestova destroyed by fire

Sep 9	Four barns destroyed by fire in Gilpin and one in Salmo
Sep 10	Three barns destroyed by fire in Gilpin
Sep 11	Shoreacres dwelling destroyed by fire
Sep 11	Gilpin barn destroyed by fire
Sep 14	Shoreacres dwelling destroyed by fire
Sep 23	Two vacant former Japanese schools near Slocan City destroyed by fire
Sep 23	Buddhist temple in Japanese camp in Slocan City destroyed by fire
Oct 5	Shoreacres no. 2 village destroyed by fire
Oct 9	Shoreacres dwelling destroyed by fire
Oct 10	Taghum planer mill destroyed by fire
Oct 14	Grand Forks barn destroyed by fire
Oct 14	Grand Forks auto destroyed in Krestova
Oct 18	Glade barn destroyed by fire
Oct 31	Hill Siding school in New Denver – attempted arson
Nov 19	Fruitova school near Grand Forks – attempted arson

1948

Jan 6	Blueberry school destroyed by fire
Jan 7	Robson community church – attempted arson
Mar 20	USCC building destroyed by arson
May 26	Krestova meeting house destroyed by fire
Jun 6	Dwelling destroyed by arson
Oct 23	Peter Maloff attempted burning of a truck
Dec 3	Slocan Park dwelling – attempted arson

1949

Mar 23	Slocan Park dwelling – attempted arson
Apr 17	Verigin's tomb dynamited
Apr 24	Tarrys school destroyed by fire
Apr 24	Grand Forks warehouse and store destroyed by fire
Apr 24	Grand Forks packing house and storeroom destroyed by fire
Jun 6	Anglican church in Hilliers destroyed by fire
Jun 6	CPR station in Oliver – attempted arson
Jun 19	Rock crusher plant in Bonnington destroyed by fire
Jun 25	Roman Catholic church in Rutland destroyed by fire
Jun 25	Glenmore irrigation district office destroyed by fire
Jun 25	Glenmore railway bridge destroyed by fire
Jul 9	CPR station in Shoreacres – attempted arson
Jul 16	CPR station in Osoyoos – attempted arson

Oct 24   West Kootenay Power and Light line dynamited near Castlegar
Nov 18   CPR tracks and switch at Kinnaird – dynamite attempt
Nov 21   CPR culvert near Glade – dynamite attempt
Nov 29   CPR right of way near Taghum damaged by explosion
Dec 4   Krestova dwelling destroyed by fire
Dec 6   Goose Creek dwelling destroyed by fire

1950
Apr 4   John Verigin's residence in Brilliant damaged by fire
May 14   CPR bridge dynamited east of Grand Forks
May 21   CPR shelter station in Poupore – attempted arson
Jun 3   CPR passing track in Shoreacres dynamited
Jun 17   Great Northern Railway (GNR) bridge near Nelson – attempted arson
Jul 8   Bridge in Salmo – attempted arson

1951
May 27   CPR tracks dynamited near Rossland
Jun 30   CPR tracks dynamited near Castlegar
Jul 14   West Kootenay Power and Light power line dynamited in Poupore
Aug 12   CPR tracks dynamited near Gilpin
Aug 26   Five transmission poles dynamited in Trail
Dec 11   Community hall in Gilpin destroyed by fire

1952
Jan 28   USCC Doukhobor hall in Brilliant destroyed by fire
Feb 9   GNR wooden trestle near Grand Forks destroyed by fire
Jun 14   Planing mill near Brilliant destroyed by fire
July 28   Pipe factory in Kinnaird destroyed by fire
Aug 2   Castlegar high school destroyed by fire
Aug 31   Dwelling in Castlegar destroyed by fire
Sep 8   USCC community hall – attempted arson
Sep 10   GNR bridge dynamited
Sep 28   Store and residence in Winlaw destroyed by fire
Oct 11   Barn in Grand Forks destroyed by fire
Oct 29   Appledale hall destroyed by fire
Nov 1   Krestova hall destroyed by fire
Nov 25   Gilpin garage, two autos, and bathhouse destroyed by fire
Nov 29   Power pole in Taghum dynamited
Dec 24   Power poles in Blewett dynamited

1953

Jan 5	More power poles in Blewett dynamited
Apr 11	Three houses in Appledale destroyed by fire
Apr 11	Two houses in Appledale – attempted arson
Apr 11	Five houses in Perry Siding destroyed by fire
Apr 11	Two buildings in Shoreacres destroyed by fire
Apr 12	Two buildings in Winlaw destroyed by fire
Apr 13	Appledale hall destroyed by fire
Apr 13	Two dwellings in Glade destroyed by fire
Apr 17	Three dwellings in Krestova destroyed by fire
May 25	Power pole near Nelson dynamited
Jun 14	Fifteen houses and Doukhobor hall in Goose Creek destroyed by fire
Jun 14	House in Winlaw destroyed by fire
Jun 14	House in Appledale destroyed by fire
Jun 14	House in Perry Siding destroyed by fire
Jun 14	Eight houses in Goose Creek destroyed by fire
Jun 14	Four houses in Krestova destroyed by fire
Jun 27	House in Krestova destroyed by fire
Jun 27	Two houses in Winlaw destroyed by fire
Jun 27	Two houses in Goose Creek destroyed by fire
Jun 30	Dwelling in Gilpin destroyed by fire
Jul 21	House in Krestova destroyed by fire
Jul 21	Four houses in Goose Creek destroyed by fire
Jul 30	Dwelling in Gilpin destroyed by fire
Aug 5	Dwelling in Gilpin destroyed by fire
Aug 6	Two dwellings in Krestova destroyed by fire
Aug 16	Dwelling in Krestova destroyed by fire
Sep 5	CPR rail line near Carmi dynamited
Sep 8	CPR rail line near Boundary substation dynamited
Sep 12	Two dwellings in Krestova destroyed by fire
Sep 12	Two dwellings in Goose Creek destroyed by fire
Sep 13	Dwelling in Glade destroyed by fire
Sep 15	Eight dwellings in Gilpin destroyed by fire
Sep 20–Nov 23	Numerous unexploded bombs found attached to power poles and rail lines throughout the Kootenays
Dec 25	Emmett Gulley's house – attempted arson

1954

May 1	CPR track dynamited near Appledale
May 1	Two power poles dynamited near Boundary substation

1955-56
Nil

1957
Apr 8   Dynamite found on rail line near Brilliant
May 5   Power pole dynamited near Glade
Dec 17   Gas pipeline near Thrums dynamited

1958
May 11   Power pole dynamited between Nelson and Salmo
May 25   Power pole dynamited near Rossland
May 25   Power pole dynamited near Tarrys school
May 25   Greyhound bus depot in Nelson – explosion in locker
May 27   John Lebedoff's home in Wyndell destroyed by fire
May 28   Dwelling in Wyndell destroyed by fire
Jun 7   Gas pipeline damaged by explosion
Jun 28   Unexploded bomb found on Kelowna ferry
Jun 28   Similar unexploded bomb found in beer parlor of Allison
           Hotel in Vernon
Jul 21   Power pole near Nelson dynamited
Aug 14   Post offices in Osooyos, Oliver, and Vernon were dyna-
           mited

1959
April 30   Unexploded bomb found on power poles, railway tracks
Jun 30   Unexploded bomb found on power poles, railway tracks
Oct 18   Unexploded bomb found attached to porch of Magistrate
           Evans' neighbour
Oct 19   Railway line near Thrums dynamited

1960
Jan 27   RCMP building in Nelson dynamited
Mar 5   Unexploded bomb found in building supply store in
           Castlegar
Apr 2   Department store in Castlegar dynamited
May 30   Planer mill in Brilliant dynamited
Jul 2   USCC hall in Grand Forks – attempted arson
Aug 25   CPR tracks near Thrums dynamited

1961
Jan 1   Dwelling in Gilpin destroyed by fire

Apr 3   CPR tracks near Grand Forks dynamited

Apr 14   Grain elevator in Wynndel dynamited

Apr 14   Unexploded bomb found at Anglican Church in Wynndel

Apr 14   Power poles near Castlegar dynamited

Apr 16   Eleven vehicles owned by Sons of Freedom destroyed by fire

May 5   Unexploded bomb found in Trail post office

May 6   Department store in Trail – explosion in fabric department

May 6   Power poles in Shoreacres dynamited

May 6   CPR tracks near Appledale dynamited

May 7   CPR tracks near Grand Forks dynamited

May 23   Dwelling in Winlaw destroyed by fire

Jun 6   Auto destroyed by fire in Winlaw

Jun 11   Auto destroyed by fire in Pass Creek

Jun 11   Power transformer near Grand Forks dynamited

Jun 17   Dwelling in Taghum – attempted arson

Jun 25   Three empty homes in Krestova destroyed by fire

Jul 3   Community hall in Gilpin destroyed by fire

Jul 30   Steps at Verigin's tomb damaged by explosion

Jul 30   Unexploded bombs were found at Pass Creek and Ootischenia halls

Sep 2   Incendiary devices found attached to dwellings in Raspberry Village

Sep 17   Barn destroyed by fire in Rasberry Village

Oct 21   Sawmill in Trail destroyed by fire

Oct 26   Barn in Grand Forks damaged by explosion

Nov 22   Power poles in Genelle and Slocan Park dynamited

Nov 22   Winlaw hall destroyed by fire

1962

Jan 4   New Denver dormitory dynamited

Jan 26   Unused Roman Catholic church in Appledale destroyed by fire

Jan 27   Power pole in Appledale dynamited

Feb 1   Power pole near Tarrys school dynamited

Feb 4   Nelson courthouse – attempted arson

Feb 16   Two power poles near Perry Siding dynamited

Feb 16   CPR tracks near Appledale dynamited

Feb 16   Vehicle carrying dynamite exploded killing one and injuring three others

Feb 25   Dwelling in Krestova destroyed by fire

Mar 6	Transmission line pylon near Kootenay Lake dynamited
Mar 31	Power pole near in Shoreacres dynamited
Apr 17	Gas line near Billings dynamited
Apr 24	Gas line near Glade dynamited
Apr 25	CPR tracks near Winlaw dynamited
Apr 28	Gas line near road to Gilpin dynamited
Jun 7	Sons of Freedom inmates in Nelson set several fires to building
Jun 8	Thirty-eight dwellings in Krestova destroyed by fire
Jun 8	Dwelling in Winlaw destroyed by fire
Jun 8	Nine dwellings in Shoreacres destroyed by fire
Jun 9	Three communal villages in Glade destroyed by fire
Jun 10	Thirteen women entered J.J. Verigin's home – attempted arson
Jun 15	Four dwellings in Gilpin destroyed by fire
Jun 16	Dwellings destroyed in Krestova, Goose Creek, Winlaw, etc.
Jun 19	Dwellings destroyed in Krestova, Goose Creek, Winlaw, etc.
Jun 22	Dwellings destroyed in Krestova, Goose Creek, Winlaw, etc.
Jun 23	Dwellings destroyed in Krestova, Goose Creek, Winlaw, etc.
Jun 24	Dwellings destroyed in Krestova, Goose Creek, Winlaw, etc.
Jun 25	Dwellings destroyed in Krestova, Goose Creek, Winlaw, etc.
Jun 26	Dwellings destroyed in Krestova, Goose Creek, Winlaw, etc.
Jun 27	Dwellings destroyed in Krestova, Goose Creek, Winlaw, etc.
Jul 4	Dwellings destroyed in Krestova, Goose Creek, Winlaw, etc.
Jul 7	Dwellings destroyed in Krestova, Goose Creek, Winlaw, etc.
Jul 17	BC Gov't ferry (*MV Chinook*) in Tsawwassen dynamited
Jul 19	Twenty-nine dwellings in Winlaw destroyed by fire
Jul 29	Hotel in Kelowna dynamited
Jul 30	USCC hall in Grand Forks damaged by fire
Sep 2	Commencement of Sons of Freedom trek to Agassiz – 700 participated
Sep 9	Kettle Valley bridge near Grand Forks dynamited
Sep 16	Bulk oil plant in Grand Forks dynamited

1963

Oct 1	BC Hydro power pylon near Matsqui dynamited

1964

Feb 12	Meeting hall in Krestova destroyed by fire
Oct 19	BC Hydro power pylon outside of Agassiz Mountain Prison dynamited

1965-69
Nil

1970

Mar 4	Dwelling in Agassiz destroyed by fire
Mar 4	Second dwelling in Agassiz destroyed by fire
Jun 28	J.J. Verigin residence destroyed by fire
Aug 30	Krestova hall (under construction) destroyed by fire
Nov 27	Five women threatened to destroy Stephan Sorokin's residence in Krestova

1972

Jan 1	Russian People's Hall in Vancouver damaged by explosion
Mar 22	Dwelling in Vancouver damaged by explosion
May 16	Mike Bayoff's home in Krestova destroyed by fire

1973

Jun 1	Dwelling in Grand Forks destroyed by fire
Jun 30	Dwelling in Goose Creek destroyed by fire
Aug 6	House in Castlegar damaged by explosion
Aug 20	Russian People's Hall in Vancouver damaged by explosion

1975

Mar 30	USCC hall in Brilliant destroyed by fire
Dec 7	Food co-op store in Grand Forks destroyed by fire
Dec 19	Lodge in Chase destroyed by fire

1976

Oct 17	Memorial site at Farron (1924 CPR train explosion) destroyed
Dec 4	Hall in Appledale – attempted arson

1977

Jan 9	Passmore community hall – attempted arson
Sep 21	USCC community centre in Grand Forks destroyed by fire

1978

Jul 28	Old post office in Grand Forks – attempted arson
Sep 19	Dwelling in South Slocan – attempted arson
Sep 23	Anna Markova residence in Brilliant – attempted arson
Dec 21	Dwelling near Castlegar – attempted arson

1979

May 12	Stephan Sorokin residence in Krestova – attempted arson
May 13	Dwelling in South Slocan – attempted arson
Jun 9	Chernoff residence in Krestova – attempted arson
Sep 30	CPR tool shed in South Slocan destroyed by fire

1980

May 25	CPR train bridge near Grand Forks dynamited
May 25	Bomb discovered on CPR tracks near Genelle
Sep 26	Microwave tower in Crescent Valley dynamited
Nov 6	Unexploded bomb found on railway tracks near Robson

1981

Apr 26	Restaurant in Ootischenia – attempted arson
Jun 28	Unexploded bomb found at Verigin's tomb
Jun 29	Ootischenia hall – attempted arson
Jun 29	CPR train tracks near Grand Forks dynamited
Oct 4	Unexploded bomb found on railway tracks near South Slocan
Oct 5	CPR train tracks near Grand Forks dynamited
Oct 27	Two unexploded bombs found on railway tracks near Farron

1982

Jun 5	Dwelling in Krestova destroyed by fire
Jun 10	Hall in Pass Creek – attempted arson
Oct 10	Doukhobor Museum in Ootischenia damaged by fire

1983

Nil

Doukhobor Groups and Their Representatives

The following is a list of leaders and their representatives who participated in or were referred to during the Expanded Kootenay Committee on Intergroup Relations (EKCIR) meetings.

Union of Spiritual Communities of Christ (USCC) (referred to as Orthodox or Community members)

Peter Vasilievich Verigin (*Lordly*) – was the first leader of the Doukhobors in Canada, and he died in the 1924 CPR train explosion.

Peter Petrovich Verigin (*Chistiakov*) – assumed the leadership of the Doukhobors after the death of his father. He arrived in Canada from the Soviet Union in 1927. He died of cancer in 1939.

John J. Verigin – assumed leadership of the Orthodox group while the community waited for Peter Verigin the Third (*Yastrebov*) to appear. After hearing that Peter Verigin had died in the Soviet Union, John J. Verigin assumed full responsibilities as the Honourary Chairman of the USCC in 1962.

John J. Verigin Jr. – has now taken over the administrative responsibilities for the USCC from his father.

Representatives of the USCC during the EKCIR sessions include: Jim Popoff and his father Eli Popoff, Alex Gritchin, Jim Kolesnikoff, Jerry Seminoff, Joe Podovinikoff,[1] and Harry Voykin. Other USCC members mentioned during the sessions were Peter Legobokoff and John Zbitnoff.

Sons of Freedom

There have been a number of individuals who have assumed a leadership function over the years. These include:

John Lebedoff – a self proclaimed Sons of Freedom leader until 1950.

Michael Verigin (the Archangel) – also lead a group of Sons of Freedom to start a community in Hilliers on Vancouver Island.

Stephan Sorokin – was introduced to the Sons of Freedom in 1950 by John Lebedoff as the long lost leader Peter Verigin III and subsequently formed the Christian Community and Brotherhood of Reformed Doukhobors.

Those who participated in or were referred to during the EKCIR sessions are Mary Malakoff, Peter Astoforoff, Mary Astoforoff, Tina Jmaiff, Mary Braun, John Savinkoff and his son Peter Savinkoff, Sam Konkin, Olga Hoodicoff, Sam Shlakoff, Mike Bayoff, Sam Konkin, Nick Nevokshonoff, William Hremakin, William Stupnikoff, Polly and John Chernoff, Lucy Hoodicoff, Pete Elasoff, John Perepelkin, Peter Slastukin, and Anton Kolesnikoff and William Moojelski (who were active during the 1950s and 1960s).

Christian Community and Brotherhood of Reformed Doukhobors

(referred to as the Reformed or CCBRD)

Stephan Sorokin[2] – although he assumed a leadership role in the Sons of Freedom soon after his arrival in Canada in 1950, his aim was to reform them, and this led to the formation of the CCBRD.

Those who represented the CCBRD were Fred Makortoff, Steve Lapshinoff, Mike Cherenkoff, John Ostricoff, and William Podovennikoff.

Independent Doukhobors

Those who were not associated with the above groups but were mentioned or participated in the EKCIR sessions as well include: Peter N. Maloff,[3] Lucy Maloff, Peter Makaroff (QC), P.K. Reiben, John Bonderoff, and Peter Popoff.

Expanded Kootenay Committee on Intergroup Relations: List of Non-Doukhobor Representatives, 1982-87

Representative	Affiliation
Robin Bourne	Chair and Assistant Deputy Minister for Police Services, Ministry of the Attorney General (provincial)
Gregory Cran	Attorney General Liaison for Doukhobor Affairs, Ministry of Attorney General (provincial)
Derryl White	KCIR
Mark Mealing	KCIR
Mel Stangeland	KCIR
Ron Cameron	KCIR
Ted Bristow	KCIR
Peter Abrosimoff	KCIR – Translator
Jack McIntosh	KCIR[1] – replaced P. Abrosimoff in May 1983
Audrey Moore	Mayor of Castlegar
Mayor S. Sugimoto	Mayor of Grand Forks
Chuck Lakes	Mayor of Trail
Joel Vinge	Corrections Branch, Ministry of the Attorney General (provincial)
Ernie Schmidt	Corrections Branch, Ministry of the the Attorney General (provincial)
Jim Bartlett	Corrections Branch, Ministry of Attorney the General (provincial)
Donna Levin	Special Projects, Ministry of Attorney the General (provincial)
Ian Cameron	Ministry of Education (provincial)

Frank Bertoia	Ministry of Lands, Parks and Housing (provincial)
Dick Roberts	Ministry of Lands, Parks and Housing (provincial)
Supt. Tedford	RCMP Nelson
Insp. Gertzen	RCMP Nelson
Sgt. Tetrault	RCMP Nelson
Supt. Cairns	RCMP Nelson
Insp. Dempsey	RCMP Nelson
Supt. Eggett	CP Railway Police
H. Vroom	CP Railway Police
Inv. B. Bennett	CP Railway Police
Carlos Charles	Solicitor General, Canada
Peter Oglow	Justice of the Peace

Rules of Procedure for the Expanded Kootenay Committee on Intergroup Relations

The following "Rules of Procedure" were approved by the ad hoc Planning Committee in 8 July 1982 for use during the Expanded Kootenay Committee on Intergroup Relations.

Chairman: Robin Bourne

1 The Chairman will be in charge of the proceedings. All statements and questions are to be passed through him.
2 The usual rules of courtesy are to be observed. No speaker shall use his [or her] turn to make a long speech. The Chairman may stop any speaker who does not confine his [or her] remarks to the question under discussion. Each speaker must be allowed his or her right to speak without interruption.
3 Should there be any cause whatsoever for disruption, the Chairman shall call a recess to allow for the matter to be resolved. Should the disruption continue, it will be left to the discretion of the Chairman to adjourn the meeting indefinitely.
4 Proceedings will be in English, but any person requiring translation or explanation of statements should so inform the Chairman.
5 The subject for the first meeting shall be the issue of fire and security from the threat of arson. The question is to be discussed under the following headings:
   a. How its use began
   b. How its continued use was encouraged
   c. What must be done to stop its use.
6 Presentations on this topic may be made by any of the groups attending this meeting.
7 A written summary of each presentation and a list of witnesses shall be provided to the Chairman at least a week before the meeting date.

8 The opening presentation by any group shall be made by a single individual chosen by that group. Witnesses may then be called to provide details.

9 Prior to each witness providing information to the Committee, the Chairman or his designate shall administer the following oath to the witness called: (A loaf of bread, salt and a jug of water is placed before the witness) "Do you swear before these symbols of your faith: bread, salt and water, that the evidence you shall give to this Committee touching the matters in question, shall be the truth, the whole truth and nothing but the truth?", or "I solemnly promise, affirm and declare that the evidence given by me to this Committee shall be the truth and nothing but the truth."

10 After each presentation, members of the Committee may ask questions of the speaker to clarify statements or to ask for further information.

11 Where there is a disagreement on any subject, the Chairman may permit further statements by the group.

12 Any or all members of the Committee will be asked to offer their suggestions for action which will help resolve the issue at hand that leads to the elimination of arson and threats of violence in the Kootenays.

13 The Chairman will formulate a statement summarizing the discussion on each issue, the conclusions that were arrived at, and the action agreed upon to resolve the particular issue. This statement may serve as a "contract" between parties.

Further to these rules, an additional rule was added by the chair that he inform the witness that protection cannot be provided under the Canada Evidence Act, should the witness desire to give information that might be self-incriminating.

Notes

Chapter 1: Introduction

1 A personal conversation in 1979 with a Sons of Freedom member.

2 In 1893, through the influence of Leo Tolstoy, Peter V. Verigin, the first Doukhobor leader in Canada, encouraged the Doukhobors to adopt communism; to forego smoking, drinking, and meat-eating; to abstain from sexual intercourse during times of tribulation; and to adopt an anarchistic view of government.

3 Aylmer Maude was an Englishman who spent twenty-three years in Moscow, where he was director of the Russian Carpet Company. His interest in and enthusiasm for Tolstoy's work compelled him to assist the Doukhobors in their migration. In 1904 he published *A Peculiar People: The Doukhobors*, which describes his travels with them.

4 Peter V. Verigin was described as "literate and unusually handsome, tall and robust, but having a somewhat brash nature and an arrogant personality" (Tarasoff 1982, 14). From the village of Slavanka, his parents were sheep ranchers who had done very well for themselves financially.

5 The actions of the *svobodniki* (the Russian word for Sons of Freedom) were said to be influenced by "A Letter to those Doukhobors who have Migrated to Canada," dated 27 February 1900 and written by Leo Tolstoy, who said that "people, upon having accepted the teachings of Christ renounce violence ... it follows that they have to renounce private property also" (Translated by J.E. Podovinikoff).

6 This act was on the books until 2002, when it was finally repealed.

7 Cathy Frieson (2002) suggests that fire was a common strategy used by Russian peasants in order to attain justice or revenge, or to exert social control over those who would violate village norms.

8 The Bolshevik government became the Union of Soviet Socialist Republics in January 1924.

9 Peter Petrovich Verigin was tall and inherited his father's intelligence but "lacked his father's emotional and mental stability" (Tarasoff 1982, 139). He became addicted to alcohol and, under its influence, became erratic, verbally and physically abusing his followers.

10 Peter Petrovich died of cancer in 1939.

11 In 1923 there were 5,000 paid Christian Community of Universal Brotherhood (CCUB) Ltd. members. In 1933 there were 3,274 members, and in 1938 there were 2,113 (Bockemuehl 1968).

12 The CCUB Ltd. was formed in 1917 to manage the assets and other holdings of the Doukhobor community. The CCUB Ltd. collapsed as a result of outstanding debts to two mortgage companies. When it went into receivership the province acquired its properties from the mortgage companies in order to prevent a mass eviction. The Land Settlement Board administered these lands until they were sold back to the Doukhobors in the mid-1960s.

13 Two children died while in care.

14 See Appendix A.

15 His residence was burned on 14 April 1950, and this led to the conviction of thirty-six Sons of Freedom.

16 See Appendix A.

17 British Columbia Royal Commission on Doukhobor Affairs, Interim Report 1948.

18 Appendix "B": Statement of Commissioner at Sittings of Commission at South Slocan, British Columbia, 7 January 1948.

19 The Independents were those who had integrated into society and no longer identified with either the Orthodox or the Sons of Freedom Doukhobor groups.

20 He organized the Sons of Freedom, who accepted him as their leader in what became known as the Christian Community and Brotherhood of Reformed Doukhobors.

21 "Doukhobors: Excerpt from Premier W.A.C. Bennett's Policy Speech," which was delivered in the BC Legislature, 18 September 1953 (author's own files).

22 A personal conversation – April 1979.

23 Seventy were initially charged. The seventieth was a nineteen-year-old non-Doukhobor woman who was engaged to one of the accused. She was later acquitted of the charge.

24 This is short for the Christian Community and Brotherhood of Reformed Doukhobors.

Chapter 2: Deconstructing the Discourse of Conflict and Culture

1 The EKCIR was comprised of skilled and knowledgeable individuals living in the Kootenay and Boundary region who were "appointed" by the attorney general to assist the Doukhobors and the provincial government to bring an end to bombing and arson. See Appendix C.

2 I was disappointed that I could not find a Sons of Freedom member who was willing to be interviewed. Two members that had played an active role initially said that they would be willing to be interviewed; however, after looking at the questions one decided to decline and the other withdrew for reasons of poor health. My sense is that they were nervous about what others might think and were concerned about the effect that agreeing to these interviews might have on their families.

3 Epiphanies may be the result of a major event or a cumulative experience.

4 Franz suggests that the historical background to this practice of deception is well documented. Apparently it is a carryover from the Doukhobors' time in Russia. Although he does not provide evidence of his claim, he likens it to the objections Doukhobors have to census-taking and to the registration of births, marriages, and deaths, which he suggests had to do with attempting to avoid the Russian police (Franz 1958, 98).

5 If anyone should have been commended for his or her role it should have been Robert Ross, the young social worker who was the first director of the New Denver

Dormitory (1953-56). Many of the former residents recall how gentle and sensitive he was to their situation and how he spent all of his time managing the numerous issues facing his young charges. John Clarkson, who took over the role in 1956, was the person responsible for erecting the fence that prevented parents from having unrestricted access to their children.

6 W.A. Plenderleith, "The Freedomite Problem and Its Relationship to Public Education," in "Three Papers on the Freedomite Problem," typescript, 195?. (Although undated, this paper was written some time after the New Denver Dormitory closed, when John Clarkson, the superintendent, was being nominated for an award for his achievement.) On file at the University of British Columbia, Vancouver.

7 Ibid., 4, 5.

8 Arguably, this means relying less on the "truth," at least until we have a DNA-like determinant for discerning which "truth" has what genomic qualities.

9 Turner assumes a basic narrative progression, which includes breach, crisis, regressive action, and reintegration.

10 Discourse refers to organized systems of knowledge that determine what can and cannot be spoken about.

11 Metaphors, as Lakoff and Johnson (1999) tell us, provide clarity to abstract ideas or concepts. My proposition is that the metaphors we use when we think about conflict influence how we conceive an intervention.

12 See McNamee and Gergen (1992).

13 See Howard Becker (1963) and his labelling theory.

14 The work of Fisher and Ury (1981) is also based on human needs theory, although they use the term "interests" rather than "needs." Interests, they suggest, include recognition, security, sense of belonging, and control over one's life (48).

15 Coser (1956) also notes that not every type of conflict is likely to benefit group structure and that conflict does not serve the same functions for all groups. Closely knit groups, for example, in which there exists a high degree of interaction and personal involvement among members, have a tendency to suppress conflict. Coser suggests that, while there may be frequent occasions for hostility, the acting out of such feelings is sensed as a danger to intimate relationships. Hence, there is a tendency to suppress the expression of hostile feelings.

Chapter 3: Auto-Narrative

1 Justice councils had their origin in the Justice Development Commission, which was established in 1974. They consisted of local citizens and members of the justice system whose purpose was to look for ways to address local crime. Before I started working for the BC government I was the chair of the Grand Forks Justice Council.

2 Hugh and I had opposed the notion of establishing another commission of inquiry because it meant that someone else would assume responsibility for arriving at a solution for the "problems" Doukhobors were having with each other and with the provincial government. We believed that if the Doukhobor communities were committed (as they often said they were) to finding a way to end the bombings and burnings, then the tools available under the Inquiry Act, especially those that would be used for compelling individuals to attend, would not be needed.

3 This, they claimed, ensured that nothing came between them and God when they spoke to the government.
4 Robin's appointment to the ministry was not without controversy. In his previous role with the federal Solicitor General's Office, he had served as the liaison between the solicitor general and the RCMP Security Service, which kept a close eye on Soviet activities in Canada. The *Globe and Mail* wrote a story about Robin's group's investigating left-wing organizations across Canada, including labour groups.
5 Throughout the 1970s the Reformed Doukhobors had written extensively about the relationship between the Soviets and the USCC, which they believed had a negative effect on Doukhobors as a whole.
6 File correspondence, 18 October 1982.
7 Three of the original members – namely, Ted Bristow, Doug Feir, and Hugh Herbison – had retired from the committee, leaving KCIR core members: Dr. Mark Mealing, Peter Abrosimoff, Derryl White, and Mel Stangeland.
8 Peter Abrosimoff's association with the Sons of Freedom and Reformed Doukhobors had to do with his role as a court translator and the fact that he was a member of the Consultative Committee on Doukhobor Affairs in 1950. Given his background and knowledge, during the early years of the KCIR the Sons of Freedom sought him out on a regular basis to share their views of what was happening.

Chapter 4: Competing Narratives
1 EKCIR transcript, 28-9 October 1982, 10.
2 Ibid., 11.
3 Ibid., 27.
4 The Reformed Doukhobors were members of the Christian Community and Brotherhood of Reformed Doukhobors (CCBRD).
5 EKCIR transcript, 28-9 October 1982, 15.
6 Ibid.
7 Ibid., 17.
8 Ibid., 18.
9 Ibid., 24.
10 Mr. Novokshonoff was a Sons of Freedom member.
11 The burning of the schools occurred prior to the CPR train explosion, which killed nine people, including Peter "the Lordly" Verigin.
12 EKCIR transcript, 28-9 October 1982, 31.
13 Ibid.
14 Ibid., 62.
15 Ibid., 64.
16 Ibid.
17 Ibid., 67.
18 Ibid., 70.
19 Ibid.
20 Ibid., 15.
21 Ibid.
22 William Stupnikoff was a Sons of Freedom member.
23 Peter N. Maloff was a former Sons of Freedom member, writer, and philosopher.

24 Peter Petrovich Verigin arrived in Canada in 1927, three years after his father was killed in a CPR train explosion that also killed eight other people. The explosion resulted in an investigation that was never officially concluded.

25 EKCIR transcript, 28-29 October 1982, 97.

26 Ibid., 16-17.

27 In a later report there is a discrepancy as to whether the year is 1971 or 1972.

28 EKCIR transcripts, 9 December 1982, vol. 4, 17.

29 EKCIR transcripts, 19 February 1983, vol. 11, 14.

30 Ibid., 69.

31 Ibid., 53.

32 EKCIR transcripts, 8 and 9 December 1982, vol. 3, 36.

33 Ibid., 36.

34 Ibid., 34.

35 Ibid., 56.

36 Ibid.

37 In 1955 Judge Lord was appointed commissioner to dispose of the former Doukhobor lands. One of his recommendations was to sell them to the Doukhobors at a nominal fee.

38 EKCIR transcripts, 8 and 9 December 1982, vol. 3, 66.

39 Mr. Hremakin was a Sons of Freedom member who allegedly always knew where dynamite was kept.

40 EKCIR transcripts, 8 and 9 December 1982, vol. 3, 53.

41 John Zbitnoff was a high-ranking Orthodox Doukhobor.

42 EKCIR transcripts, 8 and 9 December 1982, vol. 3, 54.

43 Ibid., 17.

44 Harry Voykin was a USCC executive member living in Castlegar.

45 Peter Astoforoff was Mary Astoforoff's son, and both of them lived in the Sons of Freedom community of Gilpin, outside of Grand Forks.

46 Mr. Savinkoff's testimony was discounted during John Verigin's trial.

47 EKCIR transcripts, 19 February 1983, vol. 11, 32.

48 Ibid., 27-8.

49 Ibid., 32.

50 Ibid.

51 Ibid.

52 Sam Konkin is a Reformed Doukhobor living in the New Settlement near Krestova.

53 EKCIR transcripts, 31 May 1983, vol. 14, 4.

54 Pete Elasoff is a Reformed Doukhobor living in the New Settlement near Krestova.

55 EKCIR transcripts, 19 February 1983, vol. 9, 34.

56 Ibid., 20.

57 Ibid.

58 Ibid.

59 EKCIR transcripts, 1 June 1983, vol. 17, 21.

60 Ibid., 22.

61 Ibid. During the sessions there were two media reporters who were given permission to observe: one was from the Vancouver *Province* and the other from the *Vancouver Sun*.

62 EKCIR transcripts, 1 June 1983, vol. 17, 23.

63 Ibid., 17.

64 Ibid.
65 Ibid., 28-9
66 Ibid., 17.
67 Ibid., 14.
68 His mother was Mary Astoforoff, whose latest conviction was for burning the Doukhobor Museum.
69 EKCIR transcripts, 1 June 1983, vol. 17, 36. Mary Astoforoff died a short time later from complications suffered while on a hunger fast.
70 EKCIR transcripts, 13 July 1983, vol. 22, 89.
71 Ibid., 92.
72 Ibid., 99.
73 Ibid., 109.
74 Ibid., 106.
75 Ibid.
76 Jim Popoff is part of the USCC delegation.
77 EKCIR transcript, 13 July 1983, vol. 22, 117.
78 Harry Voykin is a USCC executive member.
79 Joe Podovinikoff was a former Sons of Freedom and Reformed member who is now a member of the USCC.
80 Mr. Shlakoff confirmed the details of the story.
81 EKCIR transcripts, 14 July 1983, vol. 23, 64.
82 Ibid., 65.
83 Ibid., 69-72.
84 Ibid., 72.
85 Ibid., 73.
86 Ibid., 78-9.
87 Ibid., 80.
88 EKCIR transcripts, 15 July 1983, vol. 25, 32-3.
89 Ibid., 36.
90 Ibid., 43.
91 The first Sons of Freedom witness to present information to the EKCIR.
92 EKCIR transcripts, 15 July 1983, vol. 25, 54.
93 Ibid., 55.
94 Ibid., 57.
95 EKCIR transcripts, 4 October 1983, vol. 27, 14.
96 The Doukhobor Research Symposia were held from 1974 to 1982.
97 Ibid., 22
98 Ibid., 53.
99 *Yastrebov* was the name given by the people to Peter P. Verigin's son, who was still living in the Soviet Union. However, it was later learned that he died before ever making it to Canada.
100 As mentioned previously, during the 1940s John Lebedoff was a self-proclaimed leader of the Sons of Freedom.
101 EKCIR transcripts, 4 October 1983, vol. 29, 19.
102 His prior history was set out in numerous articles in the *Globe and Mail* during the 1970s.

Chapter 5: Negotiating a New Narrative

1 EKCIR transcripts, 2 May 1984, vol. 50, 18-19.

2 Ibid., 22-3.
3 Ibid., 23-4.
4 Ibid., 24-5.
5 Ibid., 26.
6 Ibid., 29-30.
7 Ibid., 30.
8 Ibid., 33.
9 Ibid., 43-6.
10 Ibid., 41.
11 Ibid., 43.
12 Ibid., 41.
13 Ibid., 51.
14 Ibid.
15 Ibid.
16 EKCIR transcripts, 9 October 1984, vol. 57.
17 Ibid., 53-4.
18 Ibid., 46.
19 Ibid., 48.
20 EKCIR transcripts, 9 October 1984, vol. 58, 5.
21 Ibid., 19.
22 Ibid., 19-20.
23 Ibid., 25.
24 Ibid., 26.
25 Ibid.
26 Ibid.
27 EKCIR transcripts, 10 October 1984, vol. 60, 7.
28 EKCIR transcripts, 10 October 1984, vol. 63, 50-6.
29 EKCIR transcripts, 11 October 1984, vol. 64, 2-3.
30 EKCIR transcripts, 16 April 1985, vol. 69, 24-7.
31 Ibid., 27.
32 Ibid.

Chapter 6: Rendering the Past into Meaning

1 Gilpin was a community that was created in the mid-1930s by the City of Grand
   Forks and the BC government for Sons of Freedom returning from Piers Island. In
   1932 over 700 Sons of Freedom had been convicted of nudity and had been
   sentenced to three years on Piers Island. The federal government commissioned
   Piers Island as a penitentiary whose sole purpose was to house the Sons of Freedom during their incarceration. On their return to the Kootenay-Boundary area,
   given that they no longer had a place to live, a number of Sons of Freedom
   squatted on Crown land outside of Grand Forks. This annoyed the local towns-
   people, including local politicians. It was here that an arrangement was made
   with the provincial government to buy the properties owned by Knight and Harris
   on the Kettle River east of Grand Forks, across the river from Highway no. 3,. For
   most of the year this location was difficult to get into and out of. Those who were
   squatting on Crown land were taken there by truck and told they could live there
   without having to pay rent or taxes. The Doukhobors believed that land belonged to God and therefore could not be bought or sold. The community built
   homes and steam houses and planted large gardens to sustain themselves.

2 The USCC had introduced a non-fraternization policy with respect to the Sons of Freedom, which meant that USCC members were not to be seen in the presence of the latter.
3 Jim Popoff indicated that the Doukhobor participants' singing at the EKCIR constituted one of the first epiphanies of the process.
4 The lands that the Doukhobor people once owned became Crown land in 1939 following the collapse of the CCUB Ltd.
5 No known Orthodox member was ever charged with committing such acts, with the exception of John Verigin, who was acquitted.
6 At the meeting in Gilpin John Lebedoff told Stephan Sorokin that he was invited to a large gathering that was to be held in Krestova. Mr. Lebedoff had already prepared the people in Krestova by telling them that he was bringing to them the missing leader, Peter Verigin the Third, or *Yastrebov*, as they called him. This is when the Sons of Freedom came to believe that their long lost leader had been found and was now available to provide them with spiritual guidance.
7 Peter the Lordly Verigin convinced the majority not to return to Russia, and only about 200 went, nearly all of whom had returned to Canada by 1929. His intercession against the move led to later speculation that the Soviets may have been involved in the CPR train explosion that killed Peter Lordly Verigin and eight other passengers.
8 Although some might think that the notion of a curse is "primitive," if not foreign, with regard to North American culture, one need only think of the significance of "mortal sin" within the Roman Catholic Church.
9 EKCIR transcripts, 16 April 1985, vol. 69.
10 See J.J. Verigin interview in *Iskra*, no. 1918, 75-8.

Chapter 7: Turning Points of Reason
1 The sessions were recorded and the transcripts of the proceedings were distributed at the end of each session. Between sessions, meetings were held during which the transcripts were read aloud in a public gathering. This helped to orient members to the ECKIR's role and function.
2 A collection of Chistiakov's speeches was discovered in the Special Collections Section in the Main Library at UBC.
3 John Verigin's trial in 1979.
4 When the matter was raised at the next ad hoc planning session, members of both groups chastised the individual who was suspected to have driven the women to the school.
5 Copies were made and a special collections file cabinet was purchased for Selkirk College in Castlegar, where the documents were kept. Other documents were gathered from the RCMP and the federal archives.
6 During the interview Jim Popoff indicated that he had also received considerable pressure from John Verigin to stay on. It was clear that the process had taken its toll emotionally.

Chapter 8: Conflict and Terrorism
1 The word "terrorism" comes from the Latin *terrere*, "to cause to tremble," which is used in a political sense to mean an assault on civil order, most often perpetrated by a disenfranchised group.

2 There were other Russian-speaking groups with similar belief systems. These include the Molokans, the Raskolniki, and the Old Believers.
3 See Eli Popoff's description http://www.doukhobor-homepage.com/beliefs_fundamental_bread.html.
4 ECKIR transcripts, 2 May 1984, vol. 50, 18.
5 W.A. Plenderleith, "The Freedomite Problem and Its Relationship to Public Education," in "Three Papers on the Freedomite Problem," typescript, 195?. On file at the University of British Columbia, Vancouver., 4.
6 Ibid., 5.
7 ECKIR transcripts, 2 May 1984, vol. 50, 123-4.
8 EKCIR transcripts, 15 July 1983, vol. 25, 32-3.
9 EKCIR transcripts, 9 December 1982,. vol. 4, 52.
10 Although television generated its own interpretive images, the Sons of Freedom attempted to use the media to indicate how they were being tyrannized and oppressed by the provincial government, especially during the 1950s and early 1960s.
11 EKCIR transcripts, 2 May 1984, vol. 50, 41.
12 EKCIR transcript, 28 October 1982, 15.
13 *Deus ex machina* is Latin for "god from a machine." The term refers to the convention in ancient Greek drama of having a god lowered to the stage by a crane-like device in order to unravel the plot.
14 EKCIR transcripts, 15 July 1983, vol. 25, 29-30.
15 Our Western notion of conflict is diminutive when compared to those that view conflict as nothing less than violence.
16 Another influencing factor might include the pharmacological.
17 See Julia Kristeva's "Word, Dialogue and Novel."
18 D.E. Leary (1984).
19 This in no way implies that such a role is "neutral," "objective," or "detached." An intervening role usually becomes part of the conflict by virtue of assuming a presence in it.

Appendix B: Doukhobor Groups and Their Representatives
1 Joe Podovinikoff was a member of the Sons of Freedom, Reformed Sons of Freedom, and (in his later years) the USCC.
2 Sons of Freedom claim Stephan Sorokin as their "spiritual leader" and John J. Verigin as their "materialist leader."
3 He and his wife Lucy Maloff became Independent Doukhobors in their later years.

Appendix C: Non-Doukhobor EKCIR Representatives, 1982-87
1 Hugh Herbison and Doug Feir were former KCIR members who left prior to the start of the EKCIR.

References

Abram, D. 1996. *The Spell of the Sensuous*. New York, NY: Pantheon Books.

Avruch, K., P. Black, and J. Scimecca. 1991. *Conflict Resolution: Cross Cultural Perspectives*. Westport, CT: Greenwood Press.

Becker, H.S. 1963. *Outsiders: Studies in the Sociology of Deviance*. New York, NY: Free Press.

Bennett, W.A.C. 1953. "Doukhobors: Excerpt from Premier W.A.C. Bennett's Policy Speech." Given in BC Legislature, 18 September.

Bockemuehl, H.W. 1968. "Doukhobor Impact on the British Columbia Landscape: An Historical Geographical Study." Master's thesis, Western Washington State College.

Bonch-Bruevich, V.D. 1978 [1909]. *The Book of Life of the Doukhobors*. 2nd ed. Trans. Victor Buyniak. Saskatchewan: Doukhobor Societies of Saskatchewan.

Brannan, D.W., P.F. Esler, and N.T.A. Strindberg. 2001. "Talking to 'Terrorists': Towards an Independent Analytical Framework for the Study of Violent Substate Activism." *Studies in Conflict and Terrorism* 24 (1): 3-24.

Bruner, J. 1990. *Acts of Meaning*. Cambridge, MA: Harvard Press.

Burton, J. 1990. *Conflict: Readings in Management and Resolution*. New York, NY: St. Martin's Press.

Coser, L. 1956. *The Functions of Social Conflict*. New York, NY: Free Press.

Denzin, N.K. 1989. *Interpretive Interactionism*. Applied Social Research Methods Series, vol. 16. Newbury Park, CA: Sage Publications.

Dollard, J., L.W. Doob, N.E. Miller, O.H. Mowrer, and Robert R. Sears. 1939. *Frustration and Aggression*. New Haven: Yale University Press.

Dunn, E. 1970. "Canadian and Soviet Doukhobors: An Examination of the Mechanisms of Culture Change." *Canadian Slavonic Studies* 4 (2): 300-26.

Fisher, R., and W. Ury. 1981. *Getting to Yes*. Boston, MA: Houghton Mifflin.

Fiske, S., and S. Taylor. 1991. *Social Cognition*. New York, NY: McGraw-Hill.

Folger, J.P., M.S. Poole, and R.K. Stutman. 1996. *Working through Conflict: Strategies for Relationships, Groups, and Organizations*. New York: Addison-Wesley.

Franz, C. 1958. "The Doukhobors Political System: Social Structure and Social Organization in a Sectarian Society." PhD diss., University of Chicago.

Frieson, C.A. 2002. *All Russia Is Burning! A Cultural History of Fire and Arson in Late Imperial Russia*. Seattle, WA: University of Washington Press.

Fruggeri, L. 1992. "Therapeutic Process as the Social Construction of Change." In *Therapy as Social Construction,* ed. S. McNamee and K. Gergen, 40-53. London: Sage.

Gilula, M., and D. Daniels. 1969. "Violence and Man's Struggle to Adapt." *Science* 164: 396-405.

Hawthorn, H.B., ed. 1952. *The Doukhobors of British Columbia.* Vancouver, BC: University of British Columbia and J.M. Dent and Sons.

Herbison, H., and G. Cran. 1979. *A Proposal for Community and Government Involvement in Doukhobor Affairs.* Unpublished. For submission to the Attorney General of British Columbia.

Hirabayashi, G.K. 1951. "Russian Doukhobors of British Columbia: A Study in Social Adjustment and Conflict." PhD diss., University of Washington.

Hofstede, G. 1980. *Culture's Consequences: International Differences in Work-Related Values.* Thousand Oaks, CA: Sage Publications.

Holt, S. 1964. *Terror in the Name of God: The Story of the Sons of Freedom Doukhobors.* Toronto, ON: McClelland and Stewart.

Joy, Morny, ed. 1997. *Paul Ricoeur and Narrative: Contest and Contestation.* Calgary, AB: University of Calgary Press.

Juergensmeyer, M. 2000. *Terror in the Mind of God: The Global Rise of Religious Violence.* Berkeley, CA: University of California Press.

Lakoff, G., and M. Johnson. 1999. *Philosophy in the Flesh: The Embodied Mind and Its Challenges to Western Thought.* New York, NY: Basic Books.

Leary, D. 1984. "The Role of Metaphor in Science and Medicine." Paper presented at Medicine Lecture Series, Yale University School of Medicine, 19 October.

Lyotard, J.F. 1984. *The Postmodern Condition: A Report on Knowledge.* Manchester: Manchester University Press.

McLaren, J. 1995a. "Creating Slaves of Satan or New Canadians? The Law, Education, and the Socialization of Doukhobor Children, 1911-1935." *Essays in the History of Canadian Law.* Vol. 6: *British Columbia and the Yukon,* ed. Hamar Foster and John McLaren. Toronto: University of Toronto Press.

–. 1995b. "Wrestling Spirits: The Strange Case of Peter Verigin II." *Canadian Ethnic Studies* 32 (30): 95-130.

McNamee, S., and K. Gergen. 1992. *Therapy as Social Construction.* Newbury Park, CA: Sage Publications.

Maloff, P.N. 1950. *A Report on the Doukhobors.* Doukhobor Archives, University of British Columbia Library.

–. 1957. *In Search of a Solution (Three Reports on Doukhobor Problem.)* Doukhobor Archives, University of British Columbia Library.

Maude, A. 1904. *A Peculiar People: The Doukhobors.* New York: AMS Press.

Mealing, F.M. 1975. *Doukhobor Life: A Survey of Doukhobor Religion, History, and Folklife.* Castlegar, BC: Cotinneh Books.

Popoff, E. 1992. *Stories from Doukhobor History.* Grand Forks, BC: Iskra Publications.

Pruitt, J., D. Rubin, and S.H. Kim. 1994. *Social Conflict Escalation, Stalemate and Settlement.* 2nd ed. New York, NY: McGraw-Hill.

Reibin, Simeon F. 1971. *Toil and Peaceful Life: History of the Doukhobors Unmasked.* Trans. John D. Buhr and Isaak A. Dyck. Doukhobor Archives, University of British Columbia.

Reid, E.P. 1932. "Doukhobors in Canada." Master's thesis. Montreal: McGill University.

Ricoeur, P. 1970. *Freud and Philosophy: An Essay on Interpretation*. Trans. D. Savage. New Haven: Yale University Press.

Seidman, S., ed. 1995. *The Postmodern Turn: New Perspectives on Social Theory*. New York: Cambridge University Press.

Shulman, A. 1952. "The Personality Characteristics and Psychological Problems of the Doukhobors." In *The Doukhobors of British Columbia,* ed. H.B. Hawthorn, 136-74. Vancouver, BC: University of British Columbia and J.M. Dent and Sons.

Simmel, G. 1955. *Conflict: The Web of Group Affiliation*. Trans. Kurt Wolff. Glencoe, IL: Free Press.

Sullivan, H. 1948. Interim Report to his Honour the Lieutenant Govenor in Council from the Commission of Doukhobor Affairs. Unpublished typescript.

Szasz, T.S. 1970. *The Manufacture of Madness: A Comparative Study of the Inquisition and the Mental Health Movement*. New York, NY: Harper Row.

Tajfel, H., ed. 1978. *Differentiation between Social Groups: Studies in the Social Psychology of Intergroup Relations*. European Monographs in Social Psychology 14. London/New York: Academic Press, in cooperation with the European Association of Experimental Social Psychology.

Tajfel, H., and J.C. Turner. 1986. "The Social Identity Theory of Intergroup Behavior." In *Psychology of Intergroup Relations,* ed. S. Worchel and W. G. Austin, 7-24. Chicago: Nelson-Hall Publishers.

Tarasoff, K. 1963. *In Search of Brotherhood*. Unpublished manuscript.

–. 1969. *A Pictoral History of the Doukhobors*. Saskatoon, SK: Modern Press.

–. 1982. *Plakun Trava: The Doukhobors*. Grand Forks, BC: Mir Publications Society.

Tjosvold, D. 1991. *The Conflict-Positive Organization: Stimulate Diversity and Create Unity*. Reading, MA: Addison-Wesley.

Turner, J.C., M.A. Hogg, P.J. Oakes, S.D. Reicher, and M.S. Wetherell. 1987. *Rediscovering the Social Group: A Self-Categorization Theory*. Oxford: Blackwell.

Turner, V. 1980. "Social Dramas and Stories about Them." *Critical Inquiry* 7: 141-68.

White, M., and D. Epston. 1990. *Narrative Means to Therapeutic Ends*. New York: N.W. Norton and Co.

Winslade, J., and G. Monk. 2000. *Narrative Mediation*. San Francisco, CA: Jossey-Bass.

Woodcock, G., and I. Avakumovic. 1968. *The Doukhobors*. Toronto: Oxford University Press.

Wright, J.F.C. 1940. *Slava Bohu: The Story of the Doukhobors*. Toronto, ON: Farran and Rinehart.

Yerbury, J.C. 1984. "'Sons of Freedom' Doukhobors and the Canadian State," *Canadian Ethnic Studies* 16 (2): 47-70.

Zubek, J.P., and P.A. Solberg. 1952. *Doukhobors at War*. Toronto: Ryerson Press.

Index

Printed and bound in Canada by Friesens
Set in Stone by Artegraphica Design Co. Ltd.
Copy editor: Joanne Richardson
Proofreader: Megan Brand
Indexer: David Luljak